AF600629

THE CATHOLIC UNIVERSITY OF AMERICA
CANON LAW STUDIES
No. 155

THE OBLIGATION OF THE MISSA PRO POPULO

AN HISTORICAL SYNOPSIS AND COMMENTARY

BY THE

REVEREND THOMAS A. DONNELLAN, A.B., J.C.L.

Priest of the Archdiocese of New York

A DISSERTATION

Submitted to the Faculty of Canon Law of the Catholic University of America in Partial Fulfillment of the Requirements for the Degree of Doctor of Canon Law

THE CATHOLIC UNIVERSITY OF AMERICA PRESS
WASHINGTON, D. C.
1942

NIHIL OBSTAT:
EDUARDUS ROELKER, S.T.D., J.C.D.
Censor Deputatus
Washingtonii, die XII Maii, 1942.

IMPRIMATUR:
✠FRANCISCUS J. SPELLMAN, D.D.
Archiepiscopus Neo-Eborac
Neo-Eboraci, die XV Maii, 1942.

MURRAY & HEISTER, WASHINGTON, D. C.
Printed in the United States of America

To

My Mother, Father and Sister

TABLE OF CONTENTS

FOREWORD

THE pastoral office is of the utmost importance in the Church. The shepherd of souls exercises an office which carries with it grave responsibility. The *cura animarum* comprehends principally the offering of the Holy Sacrifice of the Mass, the administration of the sacraments and the dispensing of other spiritual aids for the religious instruction and for the sanctification of the faithful. Prominent among these responsibilities is the duty of the pastor to pray for the people committed to his care and particularly the personal obligation incumbent upon him to apply to them the merits of the Eternal Sacrifice.

This dissertation is an historico-canonical treatise on the obligation of the *missa pro populo.* Its purpose is twofold: first, to trace the indications of the recognition of this obligation in the early history of the Church, and at the same time to evaluate the canonical legislation on the subject issued prior to the Code of Canon Law; second, to comment on the nature, the subjects and the circumstances of the obligation as laid down in the present legislation.

A fitting indication of the importance of this obligation is found in the number of Papal Constitutions on the matter, together with the numerous decisions of the Sacred Congregation of the Council. The ministry of the shepherd of souls was instituted not for the convenience of those to whom it was given but for the salvation of those for whom it was conferred. Of primary importance in the salvation of the faithful is the *missa pro populo.* For this reason the obligation to offer it is of divine origin. The Church recognizes the sublime origin of the obligation of the *missa pro populo* in the care of souls and guarantees its fulfillment in her legislation in the Code on the subjects and circumstances of the obligation.

The most practical and most controverted questions in the matter are those concerning the legitimate impediments and just causes necessary for the transfer of the obligation of applying the Mass to another day or to another person. Under the title "Excusing Causes" the author has endeavored to clarify this problem.

The author wishes to express his gratitude to His Excellency, the Most Reverend Francis J. Spellman, Archbishop of New York, who has made possible for him the pursuit of graduate studies at the Catholic University of America. He acknowledges with sincere appreciation also the helpful direction and kind assistance of the members of the Faculty of the School of Canon Law.

PART ONE

HISTORICAL SYNOPSIS

CHAPTER I

Indications of an Obligation Before the Council of Trent

The obligation of the Mass for the people in essence is this, those who have the care of souls are bound by an obligation in justice, founded in divine law, of applying the fruits of the Holy Sacrifice of the Mass for the souls committed to their care.[1] While the first general legislation on this matter does not appear until the Council of Trent, it is possible to find before that time, indications of the obligation and of the mind of the Church in the matter by referring to the Scriptures, to the Fathers, and to particular legislation.[2]

A. The Sacred Scriptures

According to Gasparri[3] St. Paul clearly enunciates this precept in his Epistle to the Hebrews.[4] However, in these places St.

[1] Berardi, *De parocho* (Faventiae, 1887), cap. II, n. 76; Villien, "Les Cures Mobilisés et la Messe pro Populo,"—*Le Canoniste Contemporain*, XL (1917), pp. 212–222; Prummer, *Manuale Theologiae Moralis* (8 ed., 3 vols., Friburgi Brisgoviae: Herder, 1936), III, n. 254. (Hereafter this work will be cited as *Theologia Moralis.*)

[2] "In ecclesia occidentali ante Tridentinum Concilium non videtur fuisse universalis lex quae obligationem determinaret applicandi missam pro populo," Ex. S. C. de prop. Fide. *Super Dubiis De Applicatione Missae Pro Populo—Acta Sanctae Sedis* (41 vols., Romae, 1865–1908), I (1865), 389–405. (Hereafter this work will be cited as *ASS.*) Alvarez, *Algunos testimonios historicos sobre la Misa "pro populo" ante del Concilio de Trente* (Camaguey, 1931), p. 9.

[3] Gasparri, *Tractatus canonicus de sanctissima eucharistia* (2 vols., Parisiis-Lugduni, 1897), I, n. 496.

[4] Heb. V, 1 and VIII, 3.

Paul seems to presuppose this precept rather than to promulgate it. It is well at the outset to mention and examine the Scriptural texts which authors cite as referring in some way to the Mass for the people. As an example of a similar notion in the Old Testament there are quotations from Leviticus: ". . . when the high priest goeth into the sanctuary to pray for himself and his house, and for the whole congregation of Israel;"[5] and: "after that he has come out and hath offered his own holocaust and that of his people, he shall pray both for himself and for the people."[6] The first of these texts is cited by Cardinal Orsini,[7] and both of them are mentioned by Clericatus in writing on the Mass for the people.[8] Their sole value would be as an *argumentum ex convenientia.* They show how fitting it is that one with the care of souls should offer sacrifice for his people.

Pope Leo XIII, in a constitution issued in 1882, refers to the fact that, at the very beginning of the Church, the apostles hastened to lay aside all temporal cares that they might be more free to devote themselves to prayer and the ministry of the word. The Pope quotes St. Paul to bring out more clearly the nature of the pastoral obligation to pray for and to offer sacrifice for the people, particularly the sacrifice of the Mass:

> Et ad hanc deprecationem, in qua Paulus cum gaudio gratias agens Deo semper haerebat, non est dubium, quin sacrificium Eucharisticum adhiberet, quod est praestantissimum precationis genus, et cujus ille potissimum causa pontifices christianos testabatur esse constitutos.[9]

---

[5] Levit. XVI, 7.

[6] Levit. XVI, 24.

[7] Council of Sipantino (1678)—Mansi, *Sacrorum conciliorum nova et amplissima collectio* (53 vols., Parisiis, Arnhem, Lipsiae, 1901–1927), XXXVI, 465. (Hereafter this work will be cited as Mansi.)

[8] Clericatus, *Discordiae forensis atque pensionibus* (Venetiis, 1707), *de beneficiis*, Discordia XXIX, 8b.

[9] Leo XIII, const. "In suprema," 9 iun. 1882—*Codicis iuris canonicii fontes cura Emi. Petri Card. Gasparri editi* (9 vols., Romae, 1923–1939), n. 585. (Hereafter this work will be cited as *Fontes.*)

The texts of St. Paul referred to by the Pope read: "This is why we too have been praying for you unceasingly . . ." [10] and "I give thanks to my God in all my remembrance of you, always in all my prayers making supplications for you all with joy . . ." [11] Yet these texts, considered in themselves, tell us no more than that St. Paul prayed for his flock. In the section of the Council of Trent which imposes the obligation the footnotes refer to a quotation from the Gospel of St. John: "When, therefore, they had breakfasted, Jesus said to Simon Peter, 'Simon, son of John, dost thou love me more than these do?' He said to him, 'Yes, Lord, thou knowest that I love thee.' He said to him, 'Feed my lambs.'" [12] What better food for the lambs and sheep of Christ than His own Body and Blood, than the application of the fruits of His sacrifice? Yet it cannot be said that the precept of applying Mass for the people is contained specifically in this text.

There are many authors who feel that the precept is clearly contained in another text of St. Paul.[13] This classic text reads:

> For every high priest taken from among men is appointed for men in the things pertaining to God, that he may offer gifts and sacrifices for sins . . . and by reason thereof is obliged to offer for sins, as on behalf of the people, so also for himself.[14]

Of themselves these words are certainly in accord with the idea that those with the care of souls should be obliged to offer sacrifice for those souls. But more than that, it has been the opinion of a great majority of authors that they do actually contain a clear statement of the obligation of applying Mass for the peo-

---

[10] Coloss., I, 9.

[11] Philip., I, 3.

[12] John XXI, 15.

[13] Gasparri, *De Eucharistia*, n. 496; Berardi, *De Parocho*, n. 76; Wernz-Vidal, *Ius Canonicum ad codicis normam exactum* (7 Toms. in 8 vols., Romae: apud Aedes Universitatis Gregorianae), II, n. 604; Vam der Berghe, *Institutiones Canonicae* (handwritten manuscript, undated), pars III, n. 52; Arndt, "Die Pflicht der Messapplicationem pro populo,"—*Archiv für katholisches Kirchenrecht*, LXIX (1893), 3.

[14] Hebrews V, 1.

ple. In his opinion submitted to the Sacred Congregation for the Propagation of the Faith, Cardinal Tarquini says that it is to be observed that this law was not first promulgated by St. Paul in these words; but that the divine precept was presupposed by them and therefore, though St. Paul makes mention of this law, he does not first decree it.[15]

An examination of the Scriptural texts usually quoted in connection with the obligation of offering the Mass for the people leads to the conclusion that all of them, with the exception of that of St. Paul in his Epistle to the Hebrews, merely serve to show the fitness of such an obligation. The quotation from the Epistle to the Hebrews, however, certainly can be interpreted as a general statement of the obligation. The implications of the text are summed up by Pope Pius IX:

> Iam vero cum omnis Pontifex ex hominibus constituatur in iis, quae sunt ad Deum, ut offerat dona et sacrificia pro peccatis, tum pro egregia vestra sapientia apprime cognoscitis, Venerabiles Fratres, sacrosanctum Missae sacrificium ab animarum pastoribus sese applicantur pro populo eorum curae commissi.[16]

It is true that in the pre-Tridentine sources which are available, there is a definite absence of legislation ordering the application of Mass for the people by those who have the care of souls. This absence is explainable by several facts. First, the principal persons who would be affected by such legislation were the bishops since directly to the bishops belongs the pastoral office, inasmuch as the Holy Ghost placed them to rule the Church of God; and it belongs to them also primarily, because the full and entire care of souls is in their hands, only a part of which the parish priests exercise, that part, namely, which has been assigned them by the Church.[17] But in the first ages of the Church each urban congregation had its own bishop, and every city with a resident Christian community was constituted a bishopric for

[15] Ex S. C. de Prop. Fide., *Super Dubiis De Applicatione Missae Pro Populo—ASS.*, I, 390.

[16] Pius IX, litt. encycl. *Amantissimi Redemptoris,* 3 maii 1853—*Fontes,* n. 524.

[17] Leo XIII, const. *In suprema,* 10 iun. 1882—*Fontes,* n. 585.

its episcopal pastor. Hence was postulated the reception of the sacraments by the faithful from their own bishop and their attendance at the sacred services in his cathedral church. This is clearly evident from the testimony of St. Ignatius.[18] The faithful would come to the city from very remote sections with the object of assisting at the Mass which the bishops offered on the Sundays and feast-days determined by the Church. By this Mass offered by the bishop on festal days the oblation of the common sacrifice was said to be offered with and for the people.[19] These episcopal Masses were true public Masses for the people.[20] However, this practice does not constitute evidence to prove that there was at that time a canonical obligation binding even the bishop to apply Mass for his people.

The absence of early legislation as to the pastor's obligation is more readily apparent and is explained by the gradual evolution of the parochial ministry. For the first three centuries there were no parishes in our sense of the word. The bishop was the sole pastor, his cathedral was the parish church and his diocese was the parish. The institution of rural parishes, in the fourth, fifth and sixth centuries, with more and more archpriests who had the true character of parish priests, meant that the Masses offered by the archpriests began to acquire the public character of the episcopal Mass. Pastors took over many formerly diocesan duties with regard to the parochial territory. In the cities, with the exception of Rome and Alexandria, it was only by the ninth century that separate parish churches were established.[21]

On such grounds, it is explainable that a general law was not

[18] Epistola ad Ephesios, "Nam memorabile vestrum presbyterum, dignum Deo, ita coaptatum est episcopo, ut chordae citharae."—Migne, *Patrologiae Cursus Completus, Series Graeca* (hereafter referred to as *MPG*.), V, 647.

Epistola ad Smyrnaeos, cap. VIII, 1, ". . . Valida Eucharistia habeatur illa, quae sub episcopo peragitur, vel sub eo cui ipse concesserit."—*MPG*, V, 714.

[19] Leo XIII, const. *"In suprema,"* 9 iun. 1882—*Fontes*, n. 585.

[20] Alvarez, *Algunos testimonios historicos sobre la misa "pro populo,"* p. 9.

[21] Bouix, *Tractatus de Parocho* (3 ed., Parisiis, 1880), pp. 23-40; Berengo, *Enchiridion parochorum* (2 ed., Venetiis, 1887), p. 19; Council of Agde (501), c. 21—Mansi, VIII, 328; Council of Auvergne (535), c. 15—Mansi, VIII, 862.

indispensable for the imposing of the obligation of applying the Mass for the people. First, the bishop offered Mass for the people publicly, and all the people attended. Second, there would naturally be a lack of early legislation for pastors in view of the lateness of the parochial development, a lack supplied eventually by custom rather than by statutory law.

Additional considerations also help to explain the comparative paucity of early sources manifesting this obligation. The present well-developed theology on the fruits of the Mass is a fairly recent growth; and therefore it is not to be expected that laws should have been made regarding the application of what is theologically now termed the special fruit of the Mass. Further, in the ancient liturgies, special prayers were prescribed for the faithful who made the offering for the sacrifice. Since these offerings were obligatory on all in the first centuries, the result was that the faithful of each church were especially remembered as beneficiaries of the sacrifice celebrated there.[22]

The history of legislation imposing the obligation of the Mass for the people before the Council of Trent is therefore unsatisfactory for the reason that an examination of the sources of canon law yields so few positive results. However, though the legal sources are most disappointing in their lack of material, it is possible to build up the picture in other ways, particularly from an examination of the practice of the Church as seen in the various liturgies, and from a study of the various early authors, especially of the Patristic literature.

B. The Early Liturgies

It is valid to reason that the *lex orandi* is also the *lex credendi.*

[22] Anonymous, "De l'application de la Messe Pro Populo,"—*Correspondance de Rome* (Annees 1848–1850), pp. 107–125; Liturgia Sancti Gregorii Coptica: "Memento, Domine, Eorum qui tibi obtulerun haec dona."—*MPG,* XXXVI, 690; Anaphora du Seraphion, "Recois aussi l'action de graces du peuple, benis ceux qui sont des offrandes . . ."—Cabrol-Le Clerque, *Monumenta ecclesiae Liturgica,* II, 611; Liturgia Sancti Basilii: "Memento, Domine, eorum qui haec dona tibi obtulerunt . . ."—Renaudot, *Liturgiarum orientalium collectio* (2 ed., 2 vols., Parisiis, 1847), I, 17; Liturgia Alexandrina Sancti Gregorii: "Memento, Domine, eorum qui offerunt sancta haec dona . . ."—Renaudot, *op. cit.,* I, 100.

A distinct feature of the early liturgies is the presence in them of numerous prayers for the various necessities of the Church: for example, the prayers for the Pope, for the clergy, for particular benefits. All the liturgies contain some form of prayer for the people, and not merely for the people of the whole Church, but often specifically for the people of a particular church. At the very least such prayers show an appreciation on the part of the bishops, and later of the priests, of their obligation to pray for their people, and to offer sacrifice for them.

Among the ancient liturgies the Coptic Liturgy of St. Basil has several prayers for the people.[23] This is true also of the Coptic Liturgy of St. Cyril in which are found prayers for this people, presumably the people the care of whom was committed to the one celebrating.[24] In the liturgy of St. John Chrysostom, too, prayers can be found asking God to make those worthy who offered to Him prayers, supplications and unbloody sacrifices for the people. It returns to this theme several times, indicating the necessity of prayer and sacrifice in behalf of the people.[25] The Alexandrine Liturgy of St. Basil contains an incomplete fragment of a prayer for the congregation.[26] This is matched by a similar prayer in the Alexandrine liturgy of St. Gregory asking Our Lord to be mindful of the city and of those dwelling therein in the orthodox faith.[27] In addition there are very definite prayers in the liturgy of St. Cyril.[28]

The Mozarabic Rite contributes several explicit prayers for the people, which were in use in the Spanish Church. In the *Missale Mixtum* according to the rule of St. Isidore, for example, there

---

[23] Liturgia Sancti Basilii, oratio pro congregatione: "Iterum oramus te, Deus Omnipotens . . . memento, Domine, congregationum nostrarum et benedic illis."—*MPG*, XXXI, 1665; also in Renaudot, *Liturgiarum orientalium collectio*, I, 10.

[24] Liturgia Sancti Cyrili, oratio pacis,—Renaudot, *Liturgiarum orientalium collectio*, I, 39.

[25] *MPG*, LXIII, 911; Liturgia Sancti Joannis Chrysostomi, *MPG, op. cit.*, 914.

[26] *MPG*, XXXI, 1631; Renaudot, *Liturgiarum orientalium collectio*, I, 60.

[27] Renaudot, *op. cit.*, I, 102.

[28] Liturgia Sancti Cyrilis: ". . . Memento, Domine, circumstantium qui nobiscum deprecationis participes sunt."—*MPG*, LXXVII, 1297.

occurs this very clear statement: "Offerunt Deo Domino oblationem Sacerdotes nostri Papa Romensis et reliqui pro se et pro omni clero et *plebibus Ecclesiae sibimet consignatis.*"[29] In addition, the old Mozarabic liturgy contains a special Mass which the priest is to say for himself and for his subjects. The numerous prayers contained in this Mass furnish a strong argument that its application was obligatory.[30]

These texts from the liturgies have a confirmatory proving force. Taken collectively, they show a consciousness on the part of the bishops and priests of the fact that intercession for their people was an integral part of their office. Further some of the prayers, particularly those for "this congregation," "for those here present and those legitimately absent," "for the flock committed to me," and the like, suggest even more than that. From them it can be legitimately inferred that those who had the care of souls were mindful of an obligation to pray for the spiritual welfare of those souls. In addition, the practice as revealed in the liturgies was to regard the Sacrifice of the Mass as one means of fulfilling this obligation.

It can be objected that, in reality, the prayers referred to prove no more than do the prayers of the Roman Missal today, such as the offertory prayer "Suscipe Sancte Pater," the "Orate Fratres," and the commemoration of the living. The objection has some justification, for it is not wise to attempt to prove too much from these texts. Hence they cannot of themselves be claimed to prove conclusively the existence of a legal canonical obligation of applying the Mass for the people, but merely to offer proof of a consciousness of obligation which could hardly have been left unfulfilled.

C. *The Testimony of the Fathers*

An examination of the documents of tradition and the writings

---

[29] Migne, *Patrologiae Cursus Completus, Series Latina* (221 vols., Parisiis: 1864), LXXXV, 542.

[30] Missa quae a sacerdote pro se et pro subditis dici debet: ". . . ut et indignum me iam salues, et concessum mihi gregem protum pietate iustifices; . . . quo cum grege mihi credito et cuncto eluar a crimine, et ad te merear provenire in pace;"—Cabrol-Leclercqe, *Monumenta ecclesiae liturgica*, p. 283.

of the Fathers and other writers whose works appeared before the Council of Trent helps to throw light on the question of the application of the Mass for the people. There is extant a letter of the African Bishops under St. Cyprian (210–258). In it insistence is placed on the high qualities necessary in a priest in view of his office of offering sacrifice for the people.[31] Others who refer to this office are St. Ambrose,[32] St. Jerome,[33] and St. Gregory the Great who wrote to John, Bishop of Constantinople, mentioning what he felt was his own unworthiness of the pastoral charge, in the discharge of which was involved the office of interceding for the people.[34]

The writers of a later period also spoke of this obligation, particularly in their comments on certain scriptural texts. In the ninth century, Alcuin, commenting on the fifth chapter of the Epistle to the Hebrews, repeats that the office of the high priest is to stand between God and the people, and to pray to God for the offences of the people.[35] Bruno, the Carthusian, an eleventh century writer, mentions that among the offices of the priest is the duty of offering sacrifices and prayers for the people.[36]

Probably the most cogent testimony of these pre-Tridentine writers is found in the work of St. Lawrence Justinian, *De institutione et regimine praelatorum.* This writer was the first Patriarch of Venice. His observations were quoted by the Fathers at the Council of Trent in their discussion before the reform decrees of the twenty-third session received their final

---

[31] Epistola XV—*Corpus Scriptorum Ecclesiasticorum Latinorum* (Vindobonae, 1866), III², 514. (Hereafter this work will be cited *CSEL.*)

[32] Commentarium in Psalmum XXXVIII—*MPL,* XIV, 1051.

[33] Epistola ad Fabiolam—*MPL,* XXII, 611; *Commentarium in Epistolam ad Titum.*—*MPL,* XXVI, 568.

[34] Epistola XXV: ". . . Numquid antistites ad Dominum nisi pro delictis populo intecessor eligitur."—Jaffé, *Regesta ab condita Ecclesia ad annum post Christum natum MCXCVIII,* editionem secundam correctam et auspiciis Gulielmi Wattenbach curaverunt S. Loewenfeld, J. Kaltenbrunner, P. Ewald (Lipsiae, 1885–1888), JE, 1092; *Monumenta Germaniae Historica,* Registrum Epistolarum Gregorii I (post Pauli Ewaldi obitum edidit Ludovicum M. Hartmann), I, 24.

[35] *MPL,* C, 1052.

[36] *Expositio in Psalmum XIX*—*MPL,* CLII, 1228.

form.[37] In his tenth chapter, having treated of the obligation of the bishop to pray for himself, St. Lawrence proceeds to advise bishops to be faithful to their obligation of praying for the people and of offering pleasing libations to God for their sins, especially the most sacred Body and Blood of Christ. He then admonishes those who rule the people and who exercise the care of souls in the Church to be zealous in offering the sacred mysteries in behalf of their flock.[38]

In closing the list of pre-Tridentine writers who treat this subject, one should not omit Latomus (1475–1544), who lists among the duties of those who have the care of souls that of offering sacrifice for their subjects.[39]

These testimonies of Christian writers as an argument for the existence of the obligation of the Mass for people prior to the Council of Trent are not conclusive. All the citations from the Fathers and other writers are indeed in accord with the existence of such an obligation, but, with the exception of the words of St. Lawrence Justinian and Latomus, they cannot be said to furnish conclusive proofs of its existence. However, there is a thread of evidence strung through the testimonies of the liturgies and the Fathers, which shows a continuing and developing consciousness of the existence of the obligation on the part of the clergy which it is reasonable to suppose was not left unfulfilled in practice.

D. The Councils

As has been said, there is comparatively little legislation touching this obligation in the Councils that preceded the Council of Trent. A canon of the Council of Merida in the seventh century prescribes that the priest of the parish is to mention especially in the sacrifice of the Mass on Sundays those whose charity was responsible for the building of the church and those who have con-

---

[37] *Concilium tridentinum diariorum, actorum, epistolarum, tractatum nova collectio* (13 Toms., Friburgi Brisgoviae, 1901–1938), II, 822.

[38] *Laurentii Justiniani Opera* (Basileae, 1560), Cap. X, p. 878.

[39] ". . . Ex his clarum esse credo quod pro subditis orare, pro se et eis sacrificium offerre, et maxime legem Christi verbis et factis docere est officium sacerdotis curam animarum habentis."—Latomus, *Opera* (Lovanii, 1550), p. 212, 1, B.

tributed to it.[40] However, this is not precisely the obligation of applying Mass for the people based on the care of souls.

There are, however, two items of Spanish conciliar legislation which bear directly and certainly on the subject of applying Mass for the people. The Archbishop of Valencia, in 1420, expressed himself strongly on some abuses in connection with this practice. Certain priests of his archdiocese had instituted a practice of adding special collects to the Mass, or of saying a votive Mass and taking a special stipend for the Mass which they were bound to say for their parishioners. This language points rather definitely to the existence of a precise obligation based possibly on custom rather than on statutory law.[41] There is one Spanish council whose value as pre-Tridentine legislation is doubtful, since it was held during the period between the beginning and the close of the Council of Trent. Quite possibly, it may be a reflection of the influence of the discussions of the Fathers of Trent on the forthcoming legislation. Nevertheless, since it did take place before the publication of the decrees of the Council of Trent, it may be inserted here. It was the Council of Guadix, celebrated in 1554, and it clearly placed upon pastors the obligation of applying Mass for their parishioners.[42]

To sum up, then, the state of the question before the Council of Trent, it can be said:

1. The period is marked by a definite absence, in the canonical sources, of precise statutory law touching this obligation.
2. The practice of the Church as revealed in the liturgy shows

---

[40] Council of Merida, c. 19—Mansi, XI, 86; Hardouin, Acta Conciliorum et Epistolae Decretales ac Constitutiones Summorum Pontificum (Parisiis, 1714–1725), III, 1005. (Hereafter this work will be cited as *Hardouin.*)

[41] Archivo diocesano de la curia de Valencia, libre de collasions 198—as quoted by Alvarez, *Algunos testimonios historicos, sobre la Misa "pro-populo,"* p. 17.

[42] Constitucion X, tit. III: "En lo que loca a los lugares parochias donde no oviere mas que um beneficiado se digna as Massa por il pueblo alo menos los domingos y fiestos de holgar cuando occurien, y los lunes pae los defuntos . . . Pero siempre a todos les encargamos generlamente que se acuerden en el Mimento de encomendar a Nuestro Senor a su puebol, asi a los vivos como a los defuntos."—Alvarez, *Algunos testimonios historicos sobre la Misa "pro populo,"* p. 19.

that Mass was applied for the people. It does not offer proof that this was a matter of obligation, though a conclusion is probably warranted that complete disregard of responsibility was hardly compatible with liturgical practice.

3. The works of the Fathers and other writers reveal that there was some knowledge of an obligation, and possibly that custom had introduced a definite responsibility.

CHAPTER II

Legislation from the Council of Trent to the Encyclical Cum Semper Oblatas

ARTICLE I. THE COUNCIL OF TRENT

SINCE the Council of Trent viewed the care of souls as of the highest importance, the Fathers of the Council were anxious to work for the restoration of ecclesiastical discipline through a program of reform. The five popes whose reign took place during the eighteen years that transpired from the opening to the closing sessions of the Council were all deeply interested in a program of reform. Witness the words of Pius IV, during whose reign the Council ended: " We desire reform, we wish it most earnestly, we would have it most earnestly." [1]

Yet the debate at the beginning of the Council as to whether the reform of the Church should be taken in hand first, or whether the dogmatic decrees should take precedence, resulted in a decision that there should be equal attention and position given to the work of defining the faith and reforming discipline. In its disciplinary legislation the Council concentrated on rules for those who were in authority in the Church. For, as the Council says, " The integrity of the persons who rule is the safety of those who are ruled." [2] The legislation of the Council of Trent prevailed for the most part as the law for the universal Church up to the time of the promulgation of the New Code. Indeed, the law of succeeding particular councils was, in many places, merely a re-statement of the legislation of the Council of Trent, or at least was based on that legislation.

In view of the importance of the Council itself, therefore, and particularly of that section of its legislation which is the concern of this work, it is well to examine the background of Session XXIII, *de ref.* In an earlier session there had been legislation on

---

[1] Kinsman, *Trent* (New York: Longmans, Green & Co., 1921), p. 18.

[2] Sess. VI, *de ref.*, c. 1.

the residence of bishops,[3] and on the residence of beneficiaries subordinate to bishops.[4] Since there was some question as to the meaning of these canons in Session XXIII, the Council put forth a comprehensive canon on residence and the duties associated with it.

From the evidence at hand there was very little discussion regarding specifically the obligation of applying the Mass for the people. The discussion regarding this first canon of Session XXIII dealt mainly with the bishops' obligation to residence. This *decretum de residentia* was the subject of much discussion before it reached a form acceptable to the Fathers. The subject was first proposed on April 20, 1562, and a committee was deputed to draw up the decree.[5] The examination and discussion of the decree began on Dec. 10, 1562, and the decree itself was not finally approved until July 9, 1563.[6] The reason for the protracted discussion was a wide difference of opinion. Some objected that there was no need of a new law, but that the decrees laid down earlier in the Council under Pope Paul III were sufficient.[7] Others approved the proposed decree and maintained strongly that the obligation was of divine law.[8] In all the views expressed practically nothing was said of the obligation to apply Mass for the people. However, the reason for the decree was mainly that the duties of bishops could not be properly exercised without residence.[9] Several of the Fathers, in making known their opinions, mentioned the obligation of saying Mass as one

[3] Sess. VI, *de ref.*, c. 1.

[4] Sess. VI, *de ref.*, c. 2.

[5] Theiner, *Acta Authentica SS. Oecumenici Concilii Tridentini* (2 vols., Zagabriae, 1874), I, 711. (Hereafter this work will be cited as *Acta Authentica.*)

[6] Theiner, *op. cit.*, I, 199 and 302.

[7] Amalfi: "Decretum publicatum sub Paulo III servetur. Antivari: "Placeret decretum publicatum sub Paulo III."—Theiner, *Acta Authentica,* I, 212.

[8] Theiner, *Acta Authentica,* I, 222.

[9] Abbas generalis Cisterciensis: "Residentiam episcoporum non solum necessariam sed a Christo preceptam censet, cum munera episcoporum quae Christus ab eis exerceri voluit, absque residentia exigi non possunt."—Theiner, *Acta Authentica,* II, 230.

of these duties.[10] But one statement has come down from the acts of the Council of Trent that is of great significance in helping us to see what was meant in the decree itself. On January 12, 1563, the Bishop of Montepulciano, in giving his opinion, asked how would that priest who was not present pray daily for the people as St. Lawrence Justinian taught, and daily offer for the people the most sacred mysteries of the Body of the Lord.[11]

This, then, is the background of the legislation. Natalis Alexander sums up the activity of the Fathers before the final statement of the decree. The greater part of the bishops favored a specific definition to the effect that the obligation of bishops to residence was of divine law. This position was maintained by the French and Spanish bishops, contrary to the stand taken by the majority of the bishops of Italy.[12] In the light of this background and particularly in view of the words of the Bishop of Montepulciano a better understanding of the legislation of the Council of Trent on this point can be grasped.

The decree in question reads as follows:

> Cum precepto divino mandatum sit omnibus, quibus animarum cura commissa est, oves suas agnoscere, pro his sacrificium offerre, verbique divini praedicatione, sacramentorum administratione, ac bonorum operum exemplo pascere, pauperum aliorumque miserabilium personarum curam paternam gerere, et in cetera munera pastoralia possunt, qui gregi suo non invigilant neque assistunt Synodus eos admonet et hortatur, ut divinorum praeceptorum memores, factique forma gregis, in judicio et veritate pascant et regant.[13]

Another Canon of the same Session indirectly affects the obligation. It is the decree warning bishops to see to it that those priests who have the care of souls celebrate Mass at least on Sundays and solemn feasts.[14]

---

[10] Theiner, *Acta Authentica,* II, 213, 217.

[11] Societas Goerresiana, *Concilium tridentinum diariorum, auctorum epistolarum, tractatum nova collectio,* II, 822.

[12] Natalis Alexander, *Historia ecclesiastica veteris novique Testamenti* (Venetiis, 1778), Dissertatio XII, art. XII, p. 542.

[13] Sess. XXIII, *de ref.,* c. 1.

[14] Sess. XXIII, *de ref.,* c. 14.

It is the words, " since it is commanded by divine precept to all to whom the care of souls is committed, to know their sheep, to offer sacrifice for them," that constitute the first general legislation in the Church regarding the obligation of offering Mass for the people. They prescribe the general obligation; they do not definitely specify the time at which the obligation is to be satisfied. The words, " to offer " are in themselves susceptible to two interpretations, namely *to celebrate* or *to apply*. The obligation itself is not clearly limited as to subject. It is possible to raise a question as to who is bound.

Since many of the decrees of the Council of Trent were marked by similar obscurity and since, generally speaking, statutory law cannot dispense with an authoritative interpreter, the Sacred Congregation of Cardinals and Interpreters of the Council of Trent was established, and among its decrees were numerous interpretations of the legislation of the Council of Trent on the application of Mass for the people.[15]

ARTICLE II. NATURE OF THE OBLIGATION IN THE LAW OF THE COUNCIL OF TRENT

The words of the Council of Trent regarding the obligation of offering Mass for the people were actually only an incidental part of the decrees on residence. They do not give a great deal of information on the nature and extent of this obligation as derived from divine law. In the synods and councils held in various parts of the world after the bishops had returned from this Session of the Council, however, legislation was enacted which may be regarded as interpreting the mind of the Ecumenical Council. In addition, the explanations of the Sacred Congregation of the Council insisted on the fact that the divine precept mentioned in Session XXIII obliged those with the care of souls to apply the Holy Sacrifice for the flock committed to their care. As a matter of fact it can be said that the existence of that obligation never seriously came into question, but was rather taken for granted. It was in regard to what was necessary for the fulfill-

---

[15] The official collection of its decrees is the *Thesaurus resolutionum S. C. Concilii ab anno 1718 usque ad annum.*

ment of the obligation, including its essential nature, that the diversity of opinion was found.

Soon after the decrees of the Council of Trent were made known, the discussion began about what was meant by the words *pro his sacrificium offerre.* There were those who maintained that *offerre* meant merely *celebrare;* these were in the minority. Among these were such names as Suarez, Vasquez, De Lugo, Navarrus, Laymann and Possevinus.

Suarez said that the truer sentiment seemed to be that pastors were not bound to an obligation of offering Mass for their people, at least not daily. The reasons which Suarez adduced are that there is no precept or universal custom requiring it, it is not *per se* necessary for the rule of souls, and it does not pertain to their essential spiritual welfare. Hence the obligation of applying the Mass at any time is not evident, but it is certain only that pastors are obliged to celebrate or to see that Mass is celebrated on those days on which the people are bound to hear Mass.[16] Vasquez stated his view very concisely that a pastor by reason of the primary institution of his benefice is not bound to offer for subjects; however, he ought *per se* or *per alium* to celebrate in order that the people may be present at the sacrifice of the Mass.[17] De Lugo maintained that the common opinion denied an obligation of offering Mass for the people since pastors are bound only to administer the sacraments.[18] Possevinus expressed himself opposed to the obligation. He noted that some said that one with the care of souls should celebrate on Sundays and Holy-Days, and on some other days and that then he was bound to apply Mass for the people, whereas he himself never believed that this obligation bound under pain of mortal sin, since it was not evident concerning such an obligation, either from the laws of the Church or from

---

[16] Suarez, *Opera Omnia* (26 Vols., Bruxellis et Parisiis: apud Ludovicum Vives, 1856–1861), quaest. LXXXIII, art. VI, disp. LXXXVI, Sect. 1, XXIII, Vol. XXI, 907.

[17] Vasquez, *Commentarium ac Disputationum in tertiam partem S. Thomas* (Lugduni, 1631), Quaestio LXXXIII, art. VI, disput. CCXXXIV, c. IV, Tom. VII, p. 503.

[18] De Lugo, *Disputationes scholasticae et morales* (Parisiis, 1769), disp. XXI, sect. I, n. 19.

precept.[19] Others who believed that *offerre* meant only *celebrare* are Naldus, Aloysius Ricci and Marchinus, who are cited by Barbosa.[20] Their reason generally was that the obligation to celebrate Mass and the obligation to apply the fruits of the Mass were distinct and that the latter obligation could not be proved.

On the other hand, supporters of the view that the Council of Trent had merely expressed a divine obligation requiring those with the care of souls to apply Mass for them were more numerous. Among them were Barbosa and Fagnanus. Barbosa said very clearly that, moved by the authority of the Council of Trent, he thought that a pastor was bound to apply the sacrifice of the Mass for his sheep according to the judgment of a good man.[21] Fagnanus held that the opinion which was true and in accord with the words and intention of the council was that a pastor was obliged to offer the sacrifice for his sheep, i.e., he was bound to a special application of the sacrifice and its *fructus medii.*[22] Others who maintained that the obligation required the pastor *to apply* the fruits of the Mass were Clericatus,[23] Pasquiligo,[24] Bonacina,[25] Hurtado,[26] Engel,[27] and Sylvius.[28]

The particular councils and synods do not settle the point, for they employ only the words *celebrare* and *offerre,* although the

---

[19] Possevinus, *Praxis curae pastoralis* (Coloniae Agripinae, 1645), *de officio curati,* cap. II, n. 4.

[20] Barbosa, *Pastoralis solicitudinis sive de officio et potestate episcopi* (Lugduni, 1656), pars secunda, alleg. XXIV, n. 23, p. 303.

[21] Barbosa, *Pastoralis solicitudinis sive de officio et potestate parochi* (Lugduni, 1665), pars prima, cap. XI, n. 10.

[22] *Commentarium in tertium librum decretalium* (Venetiis, 1709), *de sepulturis, fraternitatem,* n. 93, p. 301.

[23] *Discordiae forensis, discordia XXIX, de beneficiis.*

[24] *De sacrificio novae legis quaestiones theologicae, morales juridicae* (Venetiis, 1707), 2 vols., II, quaestio 851.

[25] *Opera omnia de morali theologia* (Lugduni, 1634), *Missae sacrificium,* n. 14, p. 492.

[26] *De Residentia* (Lugduni, 1661) *de obligatione pastorum,* lib. I, resol. XVI, p. 182.

[27] *Collegium universi iuris canonici* (Beneventi, 1760, 9 ed.), pars II, cap. VI, p. 29.

[28] *Commentarii in tertiam partem S. Thomae Aquinatis* (Venetiis, 1726), lib. IV, quaest. LXXXIII, art. I, quaer. XVII, p. 303.

text generally refers to the concept of "offering for the sins of the people" or employs similar expressions. A diocesan synod held in Lima in 1584 throws some weight in favor of the obligation of applying the Mass for the flock, inasmuch as it orders pastors to celebrate Mass for the people without receiving any stipend for it.[29]

The continued discussion of the question is somewhat surprising in view of the fact that it should have been settled by several responses of the Sacred Congregation of the Council as early as the year 1628, about sixty years after the final session of the Council of Trent. The first of these insists upon the obligation of the pastor to celebrate *and* to apply Mass for his sheep.[30] This was repeated in responses of 1629[31] and 1639.[32]

But even among those who favored the opinion that the obligation was to apply Mass, there was no unanimity as to just what precisely the obligation included. The controverted question concerned what was meant by the application of the Mass, that is, whether the intention of applying for the people excluded any other intention or whether the intention to offer for the people and the intention of satisfying a stipend could both be satisfied in one and the same Mass.

The influence of the pre-Tridentine theologians in their discussion of the fruits of the Mass was felt in the solution of this problem. A threefold fruit was distinguished: *Most general,* for

---

[29] Second diocesan synod of Lima, cap. II. "Praecipimus item beneficiatis et parochis ut singulis diebus dominicis et festivis servandis celebrent Missas pro populo, non accipiendo ullam pitantiam pro ipsis."—Haroldus, *Lima Limata conciliis constitutionibus synodalibus et aliis monumentis* (Romae, 1673), p. 209.

[30] S. C. C., *Civitatis Castellanae,* 26 aug. 1628: "Parochi enim diebus Festis et Dominicis tenentur celebrare et Sacrificium applicare pro ovibus suis, absque eo quod praedictis diebus possint aliam eleemosynam recipere; et licet congrua sit exigua, nec aliis modis augeri valeat ad praescriptam quantitatem, nihilominus Parochi quamdiu curam retinent, applicare tenentur, ut controversia intimius scrutata, statuit S. Congregatio."—Pallotini, *Collectio omnium conclusionum et resolutionum S. Cong. Concilii* (18 vols., Romae, 1889), XIV, "Parochus," VI, n. 68. (Hereafter this work will be cited as Pallotini.)

[31] Pallottini, XIV, "Parochus," VI, n. 68.

[32] Pallottini, v. "Parochus," VI, n. 76.

the whole Church; *medium* or *special* for those for whom the sacrifice was offered by name; *most special* which was received by the priest who offered the Mass.[33] The lack of unanimity already observed in the authors who wrote prior to the Council of Trent was reflected in the post-Tridentine writers, many of whom felt that a priest could satisfy a stipend while applying Mass for the people. Sylvius stated that, although a priest was obliged to celebrate Mass for his people, particularly on Sundays and feast-days, it did not seem illicit if he occasionally accepted a stipend from a particular person who wished to have the Mass celebrated for himself. But he warned that this practice ought not to be indulged in too often, since the celebrant ought not to expose himself to the danger of violating the divine law, even though it is not determined how often he must celebrate for the people.[34]

Schmalzgrueber later added the weight of his authority to the opinion that the Council of Trent bound the pastor by a special obligation of offering the *fructus medius* for his flock, an obligation distinct from that which each priest has of offering the most general fruit for all the faithful.[35] The Sacred Congregation of the Council gave several responses on this matter, one on August 26, 1628,[36] and another on April 28, 1629.[37]

ARTICLE III. TITLE ON WHICH THE OBLIGATION IS BASED

One of the reasons for the controversies as to the nature of the obligation was the confusion as to the title on which it was based. The Council of Trent had said merely that those with the care of

[33] Bona, *Opera Omnia* (Anterwerpiae, 1723), *Tractatus asceticus de missa*, cap. I, n. IV.

[34] Sylvius, *Commentarium in tertiam partem*, lib. IV, quaest. LXXXIII, art. I, quaer. XVII, p. 303.

[35] Schmalzgrueber, *Jus ecclesiasticum universum* (5 Toms. in 12 vols., Romae, 1843-1845), Tom. III, pars III, vol. 7, pars V, tit. XLI, n. 104.

[36] Resp. S. C. C., *Civitatis Castellanae:* "Parochos, quibus diebus tenentur Missas in parochis, eleemosynam manualem recipere non posse."—*Fontes*, n. 2496.

[37] Resp. S. C. C., *In Aretina:* "Hinc non possunt parochi novam eleemosynam recipere illis diebus, quibus tenentur Missam pro populo celebrare."—Pallotini, "Parochus," VI, n. 67.

souls were bound by divine law to offer sacrifice for them. The title on which the obligation is based, then, is simply the care of souls. This was the view of the majority of canonists.

Some, however, dispute this. They held that the obligation arose from the benefice, or from a quasi-contract; hence they believed that where the return from the office was insufficient the obligation ceased. Soto had said that the obligation was based on the fact of offerings so that the pastor was bound to celebrate daily for his parish if the income was sufficient for his support, but less often if the amount was insufficient.[38] Babenstuber summed up the controverted problem by saying that the difficulty was particularly this, whether a pastor was bound to offer sacrifice for his subjects from the precise title of a benefice with the care of souls and because he was a pastor.[39] Diana clearly stating the prevailing view said that the pastor was bound to celebrate Mass for the intention of his people, not by reason of the revenue from his parish, but precisely by reason of his pastoral office.[40]

The Sacred Congregation of the Council insistently inserted in its responses a denial of the connection between the income and the existence of the obligation to offer Mass for the people. It insisted that there was an obligation to offer the Mass even if the income were slight;[41] indeed whether or not there was any income.[42] It was the latter decree that was particularly confirmed and approved by Pope Innocent XII, because of its importance. On April 24, 1699, the Pope issued the decree, *Nuper a Congregatione.*[43] In it he pointed out the circumstances of this response

[38] Soto, *De Iustitia et Iure,* lib. IX, quaest. III, art. I.

[39] Babenstuber, *Ethica supernaturalis salisburgensis sive cursus theologiae moralis* (Augustae Vindelicorum, 1718), tract. VIII, pars IV, disp. Art. III, p. 944.

[40] *R. P. D. Dianae Panormitani Clerici regularis episcoporum* (Venetiis, 1728), Tom. II, tract. I, resol. 56.

[41] *Civitatis Castellanae,* 25 aug. 1629—Pallotini, v. "Parochus," VI, n. 68.

[42] S. C. C., *Pistorien. et Praten.,* 14 feb. 1699—Pallotini, "Parochus," VI, n. 72.

[43] *Bullarium Diplomatum et Privilegiorum Sanctorum Romanorum Pontificum, Taurinensis Editio* (24 vols. et Appendix), Augustae Taurinorum-Neapoli, 1857-1872, XX, 873. (Hereafter this work will be referred to as *Bullarium Diplomatum.*)

of the Sacred Congregation of the Council. The pastors of the dioceses of Pistoia and Prato, confused by the opinions of the authors, had neglected the celebration and application of Mass for the people on all holy days, whether or not they had an income from their office. The Congregation decided that they were bound. The Pope approved and confirmed this response and added to it the support of his Apostolic authority. Hence Ferraris summed up the question by saying that every pastor was bound by the divine law to apply the Mass for his parishioners. The pastor was bound to offer for his people, not by reason of sustenance, but by reason of office.[44]

ARTICLE IV. TIMES AT WHICH THE OBLIGATION BINDS

Since the Council of Trent desired merely to make known an obligation of divine law, its decree did not specify particular days on which Mass was to be applied for the people. Thus a determination of the days of obligation also provided a matter of discussion in the years following the Council. The idea that the obligation bound to the daily application of Mass for the people was derived from Soto,[45] and most of the authors mentioned it only to reject it. The majority favored the notion that the obligation was restricted to Sundays and feast days. Included in this group are Cardinal Toletus, S.J.,[46] Barberino,[47] Bonacina,[48] Antonius Escobar,[49] and Prosper Fagnanus.[50] It is to be noted that among these authors Bonacina holds for the obligation only on the principal feast days.[51] Another point of view was held by

---

[44] Ferraris, *Prompta bibliotheca canonica juridica moralis theologica,* etc. (Romae, 1885), "*Missae Sacrificium,*" art. III.

[45] Cfr. p. 36.

[46] *In summam Theologiae S. Thomae Aquinatis ennarratio* (Romae, 1870), quaestio LXXII, art. X.

[47] Cap. X, *de sacrificio missae,* n. 17—as quoted by Clericatus, *Discordiae forensis,* discord. XXIX, de beneficiis.

[48] *Opera Omnia de morali theologia, Missae sacrificium,* n. 14.

[49] *Summa theologiae moralis* (Lugduni, 1654), examen. XI, *de Missa,* praec. F, cap. 2, p. 173.

[50] *Commentarium, de sepulturis,* cap. *Fraternitatem,* n. 93.

[51] *Missae sacrificium,* n. 15: "Parochi non videntur obligandi ad applicationem sacrificii pro populo singulis diebus festis quippe obligatio ad

other authors. They were much less definite and employed the rather subjective norm that it be left to the judgment of the individual or as their phrase reads, *ad arbitrium boni viri.* Barbosa repeated this idea several times.[52] It was adopted by Engel,[53] the Salmanticenses,[54] and Pasquiligo.[55] The latter said that it was not determined either by divine or ecclesiastical law; that it depends on the needs of the flock and on other divine precepts; and that it can be left to the judgment of a prudent man. He then added the interesting note that since the judgment should be based on the needs of the flock, the pastor of a rural parish should offer more often than the pastor of an urban parish, since the need of the rural people is greater.

Still others, evidently basing the obligation on the income from the parish, said that the frequency of the obligation varied with the amount of the return. This is the view of Ferraris,[56] and Reiffenstuel.[57]

The responses of the Sacred Congregation of the Council furnished a guide in this matter, though they did not establish a definite law. There were several responses favoring the application on Sundays and holy days.[58] There were other responses that made the distinction with regard to the income or the return from the parish: "Si pingues sint, singulis diebus; si vero tenues, saltem diebus festis." Pallotini gives a list of these rescripts in his summary of a later response.[59] A response of 1716 said that

---

celebrandum longe differt ab obligatione ad applicandum. Sufficit igitur ut in praecipuis solemnitatibus et dominicis diebus aut semel in hebdomada parochi suis ovibus sacrificium missae applicent."—Bonacina, *Opera Omnia*, p. 49?.

[52] Pastoralis solicitudinis, pars I, cap. XI, n. 10.

[53] *Collegium universi,* pars II, cap. VI, p. 29.

[54] *Theologiae Moralis Cursus* (6 vols. in 4, Venetiis, 1726), I, 127.

[55] *De sacrificio,* Tom. II, q. 851.

[56] Ferraris, *Prompta bibliotheca, v. Missae sacrificium,* art. III.

[57] Reiffenstuel, *Jus Canonicum universum,* lib. V, tit. III, *de simonia,* n. 212.

[58] S. C. C., *Civitatis Castellanae,* 26 aug. 1628—Pallotini, v. "Parochus," VI, n. 68; S. C. C., *Militen.,* 7 iun. 1692—Pallotini, v. "Parochus," VI, n. 64; S. C. C., *Pampilonien.,* 31 maii 1704—Pallotini, v. "Parochus," VI, n. 44.

[59] "Verum quoad dies, quibus parochi applicare deberent, ex benignitate S. Congregationis ea olim invecta distinctio est, ut qui vero tenues, diebus

for the judgment of what was a sufficient income the circumstances of time and place must be considered. Yet even a pastor who had a *pinguis redditus* was not bound to apply the Mass for the people every day.[60] The general rule was that Mass was to be applied for the people at least on Sundays and feast days. In a parish with a larger income it was to be applied more often, but no law obliged the daily application of the sacrifice.

The determination of what constituted feast days or holy days was set forth by Pope Urban in his constitution *Universa*. It was his list that later served as a basis for the very definite and positive legislation of Pope Pius IX enumerating the days on which the obligation urged. In the constitution *Universa* are listed only the feasts of precept for the year.[61]

ARTICLE V. CONCILIAR LEGISLATION SUBSEQUENT TO THE COUNCIL OF TRENT

The councils and synods for the years immediately following the Council of Trent reflect the diversity of opinion on the meaning of the Council of Trent as to the nature and extent of this obligation. Many of them passed general legislation on the obligation, but in comparatively few was it made definite. The first of these particular councils after the Council of Trent to legislate on this matter was the provincial council of Valencia in 1565. As it was the first, so also, in a sense, it was the clearest in its expression of the law. It is worthy of note that it gave ample evidence of a pre-existing custom of applying Mass daily for the people, providing that this custom should be observed.[62]

saltem festis ad applicationem tenerentur, et ita declaratum fuit in *Hydruntina* die 13 februarii 1639, *in Romana* 17 iunii 1649, *in Clusina* 5 iulii 1660, *in Lucana* 10 maii 1681, *in Cremonem.* 26 decembris 1692 . . ."—Pallottini, v. "Parochus," VI, n. 10.

[60] S. C. C., *Forosempronien.*, 8 feb. 1716—Pallotini, v. "Parochus," VI, n. 12.

[61] Urbanus VIII, const. *Universa,* 13 sept. 1642—*Bullarium Romanum,* XV, 206–208.

[62] Cap. VIII, "Ne populus spiritualibus suffragiis privetur, placuit nobis: fac. ap. syn.: ut ubi consuetudine receptum fuerit tam intra civitatem quam extra singulis diebus missam conventualem pro populo celebrari, idem mos in posterum observetur."—Aguirre, *Collectio Maxima Conciliorum Omnium Hispaniae et Novi Orbis* (4 vols., Romae, 1693–1694), IV, 465.

A typical canon is that of the provincial synod of Aix-la-Chapelle, in 1585, which reads, " Curati ter in hebdomada sacrum faciant, aut eo etiam saepius vel loci consuetudo vel necessitas crebriorem divini sacrificii usum postulabit." [63] Similar legislation insisting on the obligation of those with the care of souls to offer Mass frequently is found in several councils of this time.[64]

For bishops the obligation was usually made more definite by the particular councils. A typical canon is that of the Council of Narbonne in 1609: " Dominicis vero et festis, missam dicat cum ipse sit assumptus ex hominibus, ut pro peccatis populi sacrificium offerrat." [65] Other councils of this period contain similar canons on the obligation of bishops.[66] But still other councils enacted definite legislation even for pastors, making it quite clear that the obligation was upon all those with the care of souls. An example is the Provincial Council of Mexico, celebrated in 1585, which decreed that pastors ought to offer to God prayers and sacrifices for the people committed to them; for this reason the synod decreed that they should offer the Mass of the occurring office on all Sundays and holy days.[67] Other councils employ phrases which command parish priests and those with benefices to celebrate Mass for the people on every Sunday and feast day,[68] and which state that two things belong principally to the office of pastors; one being that they never cease from offering sacrifice daily to God for the safety of their flock.[69] The seventh diocesan

---

[63] Hardouin, X, 1529.

[64] I Council of Milan (1565), part II, n. 15—Hardouin, X, 662; Council of Rouen (1581)—Hardouin, X, 1228; Council of Bordeaux (1624), cap. VIII, n. 7—Hardouin, XI, 84.

[65] Council of Narbonne, chapter 26—Hardouin, XI, 19.

[66] Council of Milan (1565), part II, n. 15—Hardouin, X, 662; Provincial Synod of Mechlin (1570), chapter III—Mansi, XXXIV, A, 591; Provincial Synod of Aix-la-Chapelle (1585)—Hardouin, X, 1546; Council of Treves (1589), sess. IV—Mansi, XXXVI, bis, 884; Council of Toulouse (1590)—Hardouin, X, 1787.

[67] Provincial Council of Mexico (1585), title II, n. VII—Hardouin, X, 1660; Mansi, XXIV, bis, 1092.

[68] Second diocesan synod of Lima (1585), c. II—Haroldus, *Lima Limata*, p. 209.

[69] Diocesan synod of Antwerp (1610), tit. XVI, cap. VII—Hartzheim,

synod of Lima, in 1594, ordered pastors to be mindful of the fact that they had an obligation to offer Mass for the people on certain days.[70] The synod of the Diocese of Olumuc, in 1591, decreed that those with the care of souls should offer the Most Holy Holocaust of the Mass frequently for their own sins and the sins of the people entrusted to them.[71] Similar legislation is found in the diocesan synod of Culm, in 1605.[72]

The discussions by the various authors began to bear fruit in the form of more definite legislation regarding this obligation during the period preceding the encyclical *Cum semper oblatas* of Pope Benedict XIV. In 1631 a synod celebrated at Cologne laid down a definite hour for the parochial Mass in legislation which evidently presupposed the celebration of a Mass *pro populo*.[73] Thirty years later a synod of the same diocese issued decrees concerning this obligation defining who are bound and when they are bound, and imposing a duty on archdeacons and rural deans to see that this obligation was fulfilled.[74] In 1699 a provincial synod of Naples repeated a response of the Sacred Congregation handed down on May 10, 1681, and ordered the application of Mass for the people, making this distinction: "Si redditus pingues sint, singulis diebus; si vero tenues, saltem diebus festis." [75] In 1717 a provincial synod of Tarragona quoted the Council of Trent and decreed that all pastors who had the care of souls were bound to apply Mass for the people, the days on

---

Concilia Germaniae (Coloniae Augustae Agrippinensium, 1759–1790), VII, 1000. (Hereafter this work will be cited as Hartzheim.)

[70] Cap. XXX—Haroldus, *Lima Limata*, p. 327.

[71] Cap. VII, Diocesan synod of Olumuc—Hartzheim, VIII, 337.

[72] Tit., *de parochorum officio*, Diocesan synod of Culm—Hartzheim, VIII, 663.

[73] Cap. VI, n. II, "Quo Christifideles Ecclesiae praecepto de missa audienda facilius queant satisfacere serio mandamus, ut in omnibus curatis et vice-curatis archidiocesis nostrae pagorum ecclesiis non collegiatis, Dominicis et festis diebus Missa parochialis certa et eadem semper hora fiat . . ."—Hartzheim, IX, 746.

[74] Statutes of the diocesan synod of Cologne, part III, tit. VI, chapt. III, §3—Hartzheim, IX, 1031.

[75] Tit. IX, cap. IV, n. 12—*Collectio Lacensis, Acta et Decreta Conciliorum Recentiorum* (Friburgi Brisgoviae, 1870–1890), I, 279. (Hereafter this work will be cited as *Coll. Lacensis.*)

which the obligation bound to be determined by the Ordinary of the place according to the revenue.[76]

In the next few years several other councils also legislated to the effect that pastors and those with the care of souls were bound to offer Mass for the people on Sundays and feast days. Among these were the councils held at Munster in 1718,[77] Rome in 1725,[78] and Warmia in 1726.[79]

The period from the Council of Trent to the decree *Cum semper oblatas* of Benedict XIV saw great development in the concept of the obligation of offering Mass for the people. The rudimentary legislation of Trent was examined and discussed by the various authors; difficulties in practice led to many of the responses of the Sacred Congregation of the Council which interpreted the mind of the Council of Trent, and the contribution thus made to the clarification of the subject was reflected in the increasingly more specific character of the legislation of the particular councils held throughout the Church. At the close of this period (1733) Benedict XIV sums up the previous state of the question commencing with the Council of Trent.[80] A visitation of his diocese, made by him as Archbishop of Bologna, had revealed that the Mass for the people was not being applied by those with the care of souls. Some pastors disputed whether there was any further obligation than simply to celebrate Mass for the people, particularly when the revenue was barely sufficient for the support of the pastor. As Archbishop, he insisted that the Sacred Congregation of the Council had decided that pastors were bound to apply the Mass for the people on Sundays and feast days. The Sacred Congregation, after repeated requests, had also decided that there was never any obligation to apply Mass daily for the people no matter how great the income from the parish. As evidence of the authority with which he

---

[76] N. XVII—*Coll. Lacensis,* I, 766.

[77] Hartzheim, X, 338.

[78] Tit. I, cap. IV—Mansi, XXXIV, b, 1854.

[79] Cap. X—Hartzheim, X, 438.

[80] Lambertinus, *Institutiones Ecclesiasticae* (2 vols., Venetiis, 1789), I, 36-40; Institutio X. (When he wrote this work Benedict XIV was Prosper Lambertinus, Archbishop of Bologna.)

spoke he offered his own experience as secretary of the Sacred Congregation for a twelve-year period, during which over one hundred letters were sent to bishops all over the world affirming the obligation.

Therefore he disregarded the protests that the decrees of the Sacred Congregation had not been promulgated, commended these decrees to the attention of his pastors and in his own name, in the name of the Sacred Congregation, and also in the name of the Pope, since the latter had approved some of these decrees, he ordered all who had the care of souls in the diocese not only to preach to the people on holy days, and to declare the way of salvation to them but also to offer sacrifice for them.

CHAPTER III

DEVELOPMENT OF THE LEGISLATION FROM THE YEAR 1774 TO THE CODE OF CANON LAW

ARTICLE I. THE ENCYCLICAL CUM SEMPER OBLATAS

POPE BENEDICT XIV, while he was Archbishop of Bologna, had insisted upon the observance of the duty of those who had the care of souls to apply Mass for the people. Four years after he ascended to the See of Peter he addressed an encyclical letter to the Bishops of Italy. This was the famous *Cum semper oblatas,* dated August 19, 1744.[1]

As he himself said, the occasion as well as the subject of this letter was the obligation incumbent on every one with the care of souls of applying Mass for the souls committed to his care. The letter was addressed to the venerable Patriarchs, Archbishops and all constituted Ordinaries of places throughout Italy. However, inasmuch as it authentically declared the common law, it had universal force for proving that law.[2] As the ecclesiastical determination with universal application of a divine precept, the bull *Cum semper oblatas* has always served as a rule in this matter not only in Italy, but also in the rest of the world.[3] The Sacred Congregation of the Council has referred to it in responses to various parts of the world,[4] and has specifically declared its application outside Italy.[5]

The purpose of the letter was to cut through the opinions of authors, so that every prelate might know what had been the un-

---

[1] *Fontes,* n. 345.

[2] Bouix, *De Parocho,* p. 582.

[3] Anonymous, "De l'application de la Messe pro Populo."—*Correspondance de Rome* (Annees 1848–1850), 113.

[4] S. C. C., in *Oveten,* 24 feb. 1774—*Thesaurus,* XXXXIII, 20; in *Fessul.,* 16 iun. 1770; in *Tiras.,* 20 april, 1772—Zamboni, *Collectio declarationum sacrae congregationis* (Attrebati, 1868), VI, v. "Parochus," III, 491.

[5] S. C. C., *in Caliguritana,* 12 dec. 1767—*Thesaurus,* XXXVI, 214–218.

wavering teaching of the Holy See. A further purpose was to furnish a rule or model according to which the synodal laws on this subject might be formed.

In its introductory paragraphs, the letter repeated and confirmed those decrees of the Sacred Congregation which proclaimed the obligation of those with the care of souls to apply the *fructus medius* for the souls of those entrusted to their care, not for others, nor for a stipend. Its provisions dealt with (1) the persons bound by the obligation, (2) the frequency of the application demanded by the obligation, (3) relaxations of the law.

(1) The persons bound by the obligation. "Now our mind and our decision is," the letter decreed, "as was often defined and judged by the Sacred Congregations, that each and every one, as long as he is actually in care of souls, and not only secular parish priests, but also regulars, whether parish priests or vicars in charge, in one word, all those mentioned above, as well as all others whatsoever, even those privileged with exemptions from general laws, unless they be specially mentioned, are all equally bound to apply the parochial Mass for the people committed to their care."[6] It then denies the claim to exemption of those whose income from the parish does not afford them a decent support, or who base their non-fulfillment on an immemorial custom observed by themselves and their predecessors.

(2) The frequency of the application demanded by the obligation. "We shall be very well satisfied," the letter stated, "if those in the care of souls offer the holy sacrifice of the Mass and apply it for their people on Sundays and feasts of precept; Sundays and feasts of precept being those which the Council of Trent[7] decreed as the days on which every one in the care of souls is obliged to give religious instruction to the people under his care. . . ."[8] To remove all doubts the additional statement was made that even on those days when the faithful are bound only to hear Mass, but not to abstain from servile work all those

[6] Chapter IV—*Fontes*, n. 345 (translated by Wiseman, "The Missa Pro Populo."—*The Pastor*, III [1884], 357).

[7] Sess. V, *de ref.*, cap. 2 and Sess. XXIV, *de ref.*, cap. 4.

[8] Chap. IV—*Fontes*, n. 345 (translated by Wiseman, *op. cit.*, III, 359).

having the care of souls are obliged to celebrate and to apply Mass for the people.

(3) Relaxations of the law. Bishops were given permission to relax the law with regard to those bound, but under the following conditions:

(a) the income of the priest is barely sufficient for his support.

(b) the permission merely allows the acceptance of an offering for the Mass to be said on one of those days, and the application of the Mass on that day for the donor of the stipend.

(c) the Mass is said for the convenience of the people in the parish church.

(d) the priest offers as many Masses for the people in the same week as he has omitted through such permission.

The law of this encyclical was received with comparative unanimity of opinion. Most of the points enumerated did not lend themselves to difference of opinion or interpretation. However, the phrasing as to the times at which the application of the Mass was demanded later led to some difficulty. The Pope had expressly included feast-days of precept on which the people were bound to hear Mass but not to abstain from servile works. This rule, when applied to feasts which were later suppressed by the Popes at various times, was a source of discussion. Suppressions took place on March 23, 1797, when Pope Pius VI suppressed six feasts at Rome [9] on April 9, 1802, when Pius VII suppressed a number of feasts in France and Belgium as a result of the concordats which followed the French Revolution; [10] and again on March 16, 1818, when the same Pontiff reduced the number of feasts in the realm of Ferdinand, king of the two Sicilies.[11]

The purpose of these suppressions was the same in each case, namely to aid the faithful, particularly the working classes, in their material wants by dispensing them from the obligation of hearing Mass and of abstaining from servile work on certain

[9] Pallottini, v. "*Parochus,*" VI, n. 83.

[10] *Bullarii romani continuatio,* VII, 282–284.

[11] *Bullarii romani continuatio,* XII, pp. 1712–1719.

feasts previously of precept. After each suppression the question arose as to whether the obligation to apply Mass on those days was still in force. The best summary of the arguments on the matter is found in an examination of a *dubium* submitted to the Sacred Congregation of the Council and answered on March 28, 1801.[12] The reasons for supposing that the obligation did not bind on those days were:

1. Benedict XIV had required the application only on Sundays and feasts of precept; but the days in question were no longer feasts of precept;

2. Benedict XIV demanded the application on days of precept on which the faithful were obliged to hear Mass but not to abstain from servile work; but the requirement was not verified here, for the faithful were also free from the obligation of hearing Mass on these days;

3. The indult of Pius VI insisted that there was to be no innovation in matters concerning the accustomed order and rite of divine offices and sacred ceremonies; but to disturb the correlation between the obligation of the people to hear Mass and the obligation of the pastor to apply it for them would be an innovation.

The reply of the Sacred Congregation disposed of these reasons very simply. The *dubium* read:

"I. An diebus festis de praecepto a sant. mem. Pio VI suppressis sit applicanda in futurum Missa pro populo in casu.

"II. An sit consulendum SSmo. pro absolutione quoad praeteritum in casu.

"Resp: Ad I et II, Affirmative."

That response settled the question in favor of those who held that on the feasts suppressed by Pope Pius VI at Rome the obligation of applying Mass for the people was still in force. In like manner the question was settled for the indult of 1818 by a decree of the Sacred Congregation of Rites given in October of the same year which also added that the Apostolic Brief itself had sufficiently declared that no innovation was to be made in regard to those feasts on which the precept of hearing Mass had

---

[12] S. C. C., *in Camerinen.*, 28 mar. 1801—*Thesaurus*, LXVII, 85.

been abrogated.[13] Freedom from the obligation after the suppression of feasts in 1802 for Belgium and France had been sharply defended in Belgium where a custom had grown up of not applying the Mass on those suppressed feasts. Its settlement was inevitable after the decision of the Sacred Congregations already cited. There remains another outstanding response of the Sacred Congregation of the Council. It was a private response, addressed to Marianus Verhoeven, a professor at Louvain who had written a treatise on the question of the obligation of offering Mass for the people.[14] After it praised Verhoeven's treatise, the Sacred Congregation answered four *dubia* proposed by the author. Four points were settled.

1. Pastors were obliged to offer Mass for the people on Sundays, and even on those feast days which had been suppressed by the Apostolic indult of April 9, 1802, even though the new promulgation of this obligation had not been made by the diocesan bishops.
2. There could never arise a legitimate custom by which pastors would be exempted from applying the Mass for the people on Sundays and suppressed feasts.
3. Pastors were personally to apply the Mass for the people and they could not fulfill this duty through another, except in case of necessity and for a canonical reason.
4. That custom could not be followed by which a pastor on Sundays and feast days would apply a private Mass for a pious benefactor, and though prevented by no legitimate impediment, would transfer to another priest the burden of applying Mass for the people.[15]

ARTICLE II. THE ENCYCLICAL AMANTISSIMI REDEMPTORIS

Later difficulties with regard to the binding force of the obliga-

[13] Decret. S. R. C., *in Aquilana—Decreta Authentica Congregationis Sacrorum Rituum ex Actis Eiusdem Collecta Eiusque Auctoritate Promulgata* (Romae, 1898), n. 4554.

[14] Verhoeven, *Dissertatio canonica de sacrosanctae missae sacrificio a parochis aliisque curam animarum habentibus pro plebe sibi concredita Deo offerendo diebus Dominicis et festis* (Lovaniae, 1842).

[15] Verhoeven, *De praxi a parochis observanda in celebratione missae pro populo* (Hasseleti, 1849), pp. 4-5.

tion led to the publication of the encyclical letter *Amantissimi Redemptoris* by Pope Pius IX, on May 3, 1858. For the most part it serves to repeat and confirm the provisions of Benedict XIV, and to correct abuses which had arisen from the misinterpretation of what was meant by the suppression of feasts.[16]

Having spoken of the charity of God in the institution of the Most Holy Eucharist and of the Priesthood, the Pontiff stated that the obligation follows plainly from the fact that every high priest taken from among men is ordained for men in the things that appertain to God.[17] He affirmed that, as the Council of Trent declared, the obligation descends from divine precept.[18] Regarding the suppression of feasts, he made it quite clear that the suppression amounted only to the exemption of the faithful from the double obligation of hearing Mass and abstaining from servile work. He asserted that the Popes who conceded such suppressions never intended that any change was to be made in the customary offices, particularly not in the parish Mass which is the chief part of the public service. Hence this present encyclical was written to formulate a certain and constant norm and law which he required to be sedulously observed by all pastors. Therefore he laid down definite rules for pastors to follow.

A. Its Legislation Regarding Pastors

1. Parish priests and all others in actual care of souls were bound to celebrate and apply Mass for the people committed to them not only on Sundays and on days of precept, but also on those days which by favor of the Holy See had been taken out of, or transferred from the number of feasts of precept enumerated by Urban VIII.

2. An exception was made with regard to transferred feasts. When the divine Office together with the solemnity was transferred to a Sunday, one Mass on that Sunday would satisfy the obligation of the Sunday and the holy day.

3. For their tranquillity of mind, an absolution was given to

[16] Pii. IX litt. encycl., *Amantissimi Redemptoris*, 3 maii, 1858—*Fontes*, 524.

[17] Heb. V, 1.

[18] Sess. XXIII, *de ref.*, c. 1.

those pastors who, because of custom, had previously omitted to apply the Mass on the days mentioned.

4. Rectors (*curatores*) who had obtained an indult, reducing the number of days on which the obligation was imposed, were permitted to continue using it.

5. In the future, requests for a reduction of the days of the obligation were to be addressed to the Sacred Congregation of the Council except the requests of those who were subject to the Sacred Congregation of the Propagation of the Faith.

B. Did It Impose the Obligation on Bishops?

A point at issue even after the appearance of this encyclical was: to whom did the expression *those with the care of souls* apply? In this regard the legislation had always been general. The Council of Trent had employed the phrase *omnibus quibus animarum cura commissa est.*[19] However, this legislation was contained somewhat incidentally in the canons of the Council on canonical residence. In the same canons those who were obliged to canonical residence were listed. They were all patriarchal primates, metropolitans and prefects of cathedral churches of whatever name or title, even Cardinals; also Bishops and any subordinate *curati* and others who obtain any ecclesiastical benefice having the care of souls. Pope Benedict XIV had said, Each and every one, as long as he was actually in care of souls, and not only secular parish priests and secular vicars, but also regular pastors and vicars.[20] In the same paragraph the Pope had referred to vicars as those appointed to take charge of a vacant parish, and there perform the duties of a parish priest, pending the selection of a new rector.

Pius IX, in his encyclical *Amantissimi Redemptoris,* had enumerated as subjects of the obligation simply *pastors and all others in actual care of souls.* The norm, then, seemed to be the care of souls. This would include primarily bishops, to whom the care of souls is given immediately. The question was never widely

---

[19] Sess. XXIII, *de ref.*, c. I.

[20] Litt. encycl., *Cum semper oblatas,* §4. "Omnes et singuli qui actu animarum curam exercent, et non solum parochi, aut vicarii saeculares, verum etiam parochi aut vicarii regulares."—*Fontes,* n. 345.

disputed with regard to bishops. The scriptural announcement of the obligation, referred to by practically every author on the subject, is the text of the Epistle to the Hebrews.[21] In that text the word high priest (*pontifex*) refers primarily to bishops; for these have fundamentally the care of souls rather than parish priests. St. Thomas had referred to bishops as having directly the care of souls rather than parish priests and as not being freed from that burden when the care of souls was shared with pastors.[22] He also said that the bishop principally has the care of souls in his diocese and priests and archdeacons under the bishops.[23] Monacelli voiced the general view that the obligation bound bishops on whom the care of souls principally falls; and that not even the Supreme Pontiff is exempt.[24] St. Alphonsus Liguori (1787) took it for granted that the obligation bound bishops.[25] Others who affirmed that the obligation applied to bishops were Suarez (1617),[26] Gavantus (1640),[27] and Naldus (circa 1600).[28]

---

[21] Heb. V, 1.

[22] *Opuscula* (Neapoli, 1849), p. 293, Opus 19, *contra impug. relig.*, cap. IV.

[23] *Doctoris Angelici Divi Thomae Aquinatis Opera Omnia* (34 vols., Parisiis, 1871-1882), III, 618, Summa, 2.2. q. 184, art. 6 ad 2.

[24] "Haec autem obligatio applicandi sacrificium pro populo non solum ligat parochos, aliosve animarum rectores, sed etiam episcopos, qui dicuntur parochi parochorum totius diocesis, et quibus principaliter incumbit cura animarum, quia cum hujusmodi obligatio promaneat a divino praecepto, nec etiam summus pontifex qui est catholicae ecclesiae episcopus, omniumque Christifidelium curam gerat videtur exemptus."—*Formularium legale-practicum* (Romae, 1884), pars II, tit. XVI, n. 20.

[25] "Omitto denique sermonem facere de aliis Episcopi muneribus v. g., de Missa quam ipse, etiam plusquam Parochus, tenetur pro suis ovibus applicare."—*Homo apostolicus* (Augustae Taurinorum, 1870), tract. VII, n. 65, p. 518; cf. also St. Alphonsus, *Theologia moralis* (Matriti, 1876), I, 97, lib. VI, tract. III, *de Eucharistia*, cap. III, n. 325.

[26] *Opera Omnia,* XXI, 907.

[27] *Commentaria in rubricas missali* (Venetiis, 1774), pars III, tit. XII, n. 27.

[28] *Summa, v. "Parochus,"* n. 19: "Revera non magis debet de jure divino obligare parochus in hoc pro suis ovibus quam praelatus Regularis pro suis subditis, episcopus pro sua Diocesi, atque Summus Pontifex pro universali Ecclesia, in quibus proportionaliter esset dicendum quod de Parocho."—as quoted in Ferraris, *Prompta bibliotheca, v. "Missae sacrificium,"* art. III.

Thus it is evident that there is no doubt of the inclusion of bishops among those who are bound to apply Mass for their flock. The Sacred Congregation of the Council had issued several decrees touching this matter, the most distinct reference being had in a decree issued in 1881.[29]

C. Status of Pastors in the United States

A more disputed problem was that of deciding whether or not missionaries were included among those who, under the Encyclical of Pius IX, were bound by the obligation. The Sacred Congregation of the Propagation of the Faith had issued an encyclical letter (1860) in which it decided that Vicars Apostolic and missionaries were not bound to offer the Mass for the people. The Sacred Congregation stated that this was evident from a close inspection of the *Amantissimi Redemptoris,* and that the only reason for the letter of 1860 was to quiet the doubts of those who inquired concerning this obligation.[30] This did not affect the previous distinction of the Sacred Congregation that missionary *parochi,* those having the care of souls in canonically erected parishes, were bound in justice to the obligation of applying Mass for the people.[31] A response of the Sacred Congregation given in 1863, however, was the occasion for some difficulty for the Fathers of the II Plenary Council of Baltimore. The first part of the dubium asked whether they who received the care of souls but in some determined place were bound in justice to apply Mass for the people on feast days. The answer was in the negative, on condition that the places involved were not those in which Episcopal Sees and parishes had already been canonically erected, or to which Vicars Apostolic and missionaries had been sent to take the place of legitimate pastors.[32] This decree had its effect

---

29 S. C. C., *in Romana,* 9 iulii 1881: "Episcopos teneri ad applicationem Missae pro Populo; et consulendum SSmo. ut decernere dignetur, eosdem Missam pro populo applicare debere omnibus aliisque festis diebus, tum de praecepto, tum suppressis."—*ASS,* XIV, 547.

30 S. C. de prop. Fide., litt. encycl., 5 aug. 1860—*Collectanea,* n. 1199.

31 S. C. de prop. Fide, resp. *in Curacao,* 12 sept. 1843—quoted in *ASS,* I, 401.

32 Resp. S. C. de prop. Fide, 23 martii 1863—*ASS,* I (1865), 407.

on the action of the II Plenary Council of Baltimore. In one decree the Fathers first mentioned the canons of the Council of Trent. Then, they referred especially to the constitution *Cum semper oblatas,* emphasizing its point that pastors and all actually having the care of souls are bound to apply Mass for the people.[33] Moreover, they decreed that pastors and rectors of souls were not to regard themselves freed from the obligation of applying Mass for the people on those feast days on which the people, by virtue of Apostolic indult, were exempted from the obligation of hearing Mass and abstaining from servile work. They remarked, however, that the bishops had obtained from the Holy See the faculty of dispensing the pastors on those days, provided they prayed especially for their people at Mass.[34]

This would seem to imply that the discipline in the United States was the same as the general discipline on this matter, and that pastors were bound to apply Mass for their people on Sundays and on holy days of obl'gation, even on suppressed feasts. But the response of 1863 had given rise to some doubts on the matter with regard to pastors in the United States; hence in the subsequent provision they asked the Congregation whether that response included missionaries in this region where canonically erected parishes did not exist.[35] The request was answered on the twenty-fourth of January, 1868, in an instruction of the Sacred Congregation which dealt with the questions proposed to it by the Fathers of the Council. The answer stated that, on the hypothesis that canonically erected parishes did not exist, the matter was provided for in the decree of August 18, 1866.[36] This response of 1866 repeated the provisions of that of

---

[33] *Concilii plenarii Baltimorensis II, in ecclesia metropolitana Baltimorensi habiti acta et decreta* (Baltimorae, 1894), n. 366.

[34] II Plenary Council of Baltimore—*op. cit.*, n. 367.

[35] II Plenary Council of Baltimore—*op. cit.*, n. 368.

[36] Instructio S. C. de Prop. Fide, Circa Postulata a Patribus Concilii, 24 jan. 1868, pars II: "Postulatum quoque a Synodo propositum, Tit. VI, C. I., N. 395 accurate expensum est, quo nimirum petebatur ut S. Congregatio apertius declararet, an Missionarii Foederatorum Statuum ubi paroeciae canonice erectae nondum existunt, ad Missam pro populo festis diebus applicandam teneantur. Itaque S. C. respondit, posito quod non extent

1863 adding that Vicars Apostolic and missionaries were not bound in justice to apply the Mass for the people, provided that the places involved were not those in which Episcopal Sees had already been canonically erected and to which the Apostolic Vicars had been sent to take the office of legitimate pastors or to which missionaries had been sent as pastors.[37] From these responses it could be inferred that the obligation was not binding on pastors in the United States, since they were missionaries in charge of parishes that had not yet been canonically erected.

The general view seemed to be that, according to the decision of the Sacred Congregation, pastors in the United States were not bound by the obligation of applying Mass for the people. This was reflected in the decree of the X Provincial Council of Baltimore, held in 1869, repeated in toto in the IX Diocesan Synod of Baltimore in 1886.[38] This decree was the answer to the question of Archbishop Spalding whether it would be wise to ask the Holy See to change the decision recently given to the effect that our pastors were bound neither by justice nor charity to apply for the people.[39] Two authors of this period, writing for the United States, denied that pastors in this country were bound to the obligation.[40] Konings said that the obligation did not exist here and he quoted n. 368 of the II Plenary Council of Baltimore as his authority. Sabetti also denied the obligation for priests of this country. Both were opposed by Wiseman who insisted that

---

Paroeciae canonice erectae, provisum esse per Decretum S. Concilii, 18 aug. 1866; . . ."—*II Plenary Council of Baltimore,* lxix.; *Coll. Lacensis,* III, 383.

[37] S. C. de Prop. Fidei, Resp. 18 aug. 1866—*II Plenary Council of Baltimore,* lxxii; *Coll. Lacen.,* III, 386.

[38] Decr. VIII, "Quamvis, juxta decisionem recenter per S. C. de Propaganda Fide nobis enuntiatam animarum Pastores hac in Provincia, ubi nullae hactenus propriae dictae paroeciae sunt canonice institutae, haud teneantur, neque ex justitia, nequidem ex caritate, Missam pro populo sibi commisso diebus Dominicis et Festis applicare, attamen cum id valde deceat ex caritate eos omnes enixe in Domino hortamur ut id muneris adeo populo utile Deoque earum exsequi pergant, a Principe Pastorum mercedem magnam nimis percepturi."—*Coll. Lacensis,* III, 594.

[39] Questiones pertractandae, n. 25—*Coll. Lacensis,* III, 578.

[40] Konings, *Theologia moralis* (Bostoniae, 1874), n. 1139; Sabetti, *Compendium theologiae moralis* (Neo-Eboraci, 1884), n. 710.

" the second plenary Council is quite gratuitously and erroneously invoked as authority for teaching that rectors in the United States are exempt from the obligation of applying Mass for the people. The decision of the Propaganda in 1863 to the effect that missionaries and Vicars Apostolic are not bound to the *Missa pro populo* has no bearing on diocesan clergy, whether in the United States or elsewhere. That decision concerned only missionaries in the proper sense of the word, *qui nullae sedi addicti.*" [41] The general opinion, however, came to be, especially after the III Plenary Council of Baltimore, that in the United States, with the possible exception of San Francisco, there was no clear and judicial obligation upon pastors to celebrate and apply Mass for the people.[42] A reason was derived from the declaration of the III Plenary Council of Baltimore that canonically erected parishes did not exist in this country.[43] The exception regarding San Francisco was based on a deduction from the words of the I Provincial Council of San Francisco that the faithful and rectors of those parishes which are regarded as canonical parishes, though the rectors in charge of them are not canonical parish priests, are mutually bound by all the duties of parishioners and parish priests, in the proper sense as laid down by the common law.[44] Putzer however declared that Archbishop Alemany did not think that there were parishes properly so-called in that province nor that the rectors were strictly bound to apply the

---

[41] Wiseman, " The Missa Pro Populo"—*The Pastor,* VI (1886), 271.

[42] *Ecclesiastical Review,* I (1889), 264; XVI (1897), 188 (hereafter cited as *ER.*) ; Smith, *Elements of Ecclesiastical Law* (5 ed., 2 vols., New York, 1883), I, nn. 654, 657, 666.

[43] III Plenary Council of Baltimore, n. 24—*Acta et Decreta Concilii Plenarii Baltimorensis Tertii,* A. D. MDCCCLXXXIV (Baltimorae: John Murphy, 1896).

[44] N. XIV: " Declaramus rectores earum paroeciarum quae habentur uti paroeciae propriae dictae, teneri ad omnia munia parochorum erga fideles intra limites suarum ecclesiarum constitutos adimplenda fideles autem jus habere ad subsidia spiritualia ab illis seu a propriis animarum rectoribus recipiendum ac specialiter teneri ad ipsos recurre pro communione pasceali, baptismo, viatico extrema unctione et matrimonio." First Provincial Council of San Francisco (1874)—Smith, *Elements of Ecclesiastical Law,* I, n. 654.

Mass for the people.[45] This was also the opinion of Slater.[46] In 1909 the United States was removed from the jurisdiction of the Congregation of the Propagation of the Faith.[47] This transfer, however, was generally conceded to make no change in the status of pastors in this country, or their obligation in regard to applying the Mass.[48] Up to the time of the Code pastors in the United States were probably not bound to apply Mass for the people. This conclusion seems warranted though after the decree Maxima Cura in 1910 there was ground for the opinion that irremovable pastors in this country were canonical pastors.[49] According to canon thirty of the decree all pastors who had obtained a parish in virtue of any title whatsoever were included, so long as they were deemed rectors in the true sense of the word. When the Sacred Congregation of the Consistory stated that the decree was to be observed in both England and the United States[50] it seemed at least to make irremovable parishes canonically erected parishes. The decree did not apply to those pastors in the United States who were removable *ad nutum*.[51] However, even after the publication of Maxima Cura, the question whether irremovable pastors in the United States were canonical pastors and therefore bound by the obligation of Mass for the people remained for the Code to settle definitely.[52]

ARTICLE III. THE CONSTITUTION IN SUPREMA

The last in the series of pontifical Constitutions issued to define

---

[45] Konings-Putzer, *Commentarium in Facultates Apostolicas Episcopis nec non Vicariis et Praefectis Apostolicis per modum formularium concedi solitas* (4 ed., New York, 1897), p. 172.

[46] *A Manual of Moral Theology* (3 ed., 2 vols., New York, 1908), II, 121, also I, 630.

[47] Pius X, const. *Sapienti Consilio,* 29 iun., 1908—*Fontes,* n. 682.

[48] Gury, Ballerini-Barrett, *Compendium Theologiae Moralis* (22 ed., New York, 1915), n. 710; *ER,* XL (1909), p. 190.

[49] S. C. Consist., decr. *Maxima cura,* 20 aug., 1910—*AAS,* II (1910), 636–648; *Fontes,* n. 2074.

[50] S. C. Consist., 28 febr., 13 mart., 1911—*AAS,* III (1911), 133.

[51] S. C. Consist., 28 iun., 1915—*AAS,* VII (1915), 378; *Fontes,* n. 2090.

[52] Cfr. Golden, *Parochial Benefices in the New Code* (The Catholic University of America Canon Law Studies, n. 10, Washington, D. C.: The Catholic University of America, 1921), p. 100.

and determine the law on the application of Mass for the people was the constitution *In suprema* of Pope Leo XIII, dated June 10, 1882.

In introducing his contribution to the ecclesiastical law on the matter, Leo paid tribute to the work of Pope Benedict XIV in this regard. He also mentioned the Constitution *A quo die* of Clement XIII, which had admonished bishops to think no duty more transcendent than to offer to God the Father again and again the Victim of Propitiation for their own sins and for the sins of the people. He then listed the purpose of his letter; namely to settle definitely by a law of the Holy See the obligation of bishops with regard to the Mass for the people. Indeed he stated that up to this time none of the Roman Congregations had put forth a definitive decree concerning the days on which bishops were bound to the obligation.[58]

The points peculiar to the Constitution of Pope Leo XIII were:

1. There is no mention made of Bishops in the encyclical *Cum semper oblatas;* there can be no doubt, however, that Benedict XIV, who so forcibly enjoined the obligation of the application of Mass for the people on parish priests, wished it to be understood, indirectly at least, as prescribed *a fortiori* for pastors of higher rank than *parochi.*

2. There is but one opinion among doctors of moral theology and canon law; namely that the obligation of applying the Mass for the people is binding upon bishops by a duty prior to that obliging parish priests.

3. Parish priests hold office by ecclesiastical institution though its origin may be traced to that divine right which is called *mediate* and *hypothetical.* To bishops, on the contrary, belongs the pastoral office *immediately,* by divine institution since the Holy Ghost placed them to rule the Church of God, and principally, because the full and entire care of souls is in their hands. This distinction had not been drawn in the preceding papal letters on this matter; but its statement here was merely a preliminary to the next three points regarding the bishops' obligation.

4. Each and every bishop, to whatever dignity he may be

---

[58] Leo XIII, ap. const., *in suprema,* 10 iun., 1882—*Fontes,* n. 585.

raised, even to that of the Cardinalate, as also abbots who have quasi-episcopal jurisdiction over clergy and people in a separate territory, *is bound to celebrate and apply Mass for the people under his charge on Sundays and other feast days which are still of precept, and also on those days which have been withdrawn from the number of feasts of precept.*

5. Bishops and abbots fulfill their duty in this matter by *celebrating and applying one Mass for all the people committed to their care,* even if they govern two or more dioceses or abbeys merged into one. This is true despite decisions of the Roman Congregations which prescribe otherwise for *parochi* who preside over two parishes united into one *aequiprincipaliter.*

6. Titular bishops are not bound to the obligation of the application of Mass for the people. A residential bishop is bound only after he takes possession of his See.[54] Taking equity and episcopal charity into account it is proper, however, that even titular bishops should occasionally offer Mass for the people of their titular Sees.

Such is the teaching of the Constitution *In suprema,* the last of the papal documents devoted exclusively to the question of Mass for the people. One of its points was later repeated in the Constitution of Pius X Apostolicae, April 15, 1910.[55]

Moreover the Sacred Congregations issued later responses on the general obligation. The Sacred Congregation of the Council in 1892 denied to a pastor the right to celebrate a founded Mass or a chanted Mass on the days on which he was bound to apply the Mass for the people, providing for the latter through a proxy.[56] The Sacred Congregation of Rites in 1911 stated that even in a Church having only one Mass on Sundays and feast days the *parochus* was bound to apply the Mass for the people according to the office of the day, even on Sundays to which the solemnities of certain feasts have been transferred, rather than satisfy the obligation by the Mass of these solemnities.[57] In 1911

---

[54] S. R. C., *in Marsor,* 12 nov., 1831—*Decret. authen.,* n. 2682 ad 22.

[55] N. X., "Cardinales debent Missam, sicut ceteri episcopi residentes, pro populo applicare."—*Fontes,* 686.

[56] S. C. C., *in Melvitana,* 9 april, 1892—*ASS,* XXIV, 661-669.

[57] S. R. C., *in Baionen,* 27 maii, 1911, ad VIII—*AAS,* III, 282.

Pius X suppressed some feasts.[58] The Sacred Congregation of the Council decided that the obligation of applying for the people remained even on those days.[59]

From the foregoing chapters it is evident that until the Council of Trent there was no general statutory legislation for the whole Church on the application of Mass for the people, though the existence of some obligation, perhaps based on custom, was acknowledged. The decree of the Council of Trent while it was very broad and not specific on the subject either of the persons bound, the days on which they were bound, or the circumstances surrounding the obligation, did set a general norm for the whole Church. This norm was followed and determined by the ecclesiastical legislation which came in the form of responses of Congregations, in papal encyclical letters and constitutions and in the laws of particular councils. By the time of the Code, then, the law was very well determined and in several instances the canons of the Code repeat substantially, if not verbatim, the pre-Code law as thus evolved.

---

[58] Pius X, const. *Supremi disciplinae,* 2 iulii, 1911—*AAS,* III, 305.
[59] S. C. C., *Romana et aliarum,* 8 aug., 1911—*AAS,* III, 391.

PART TWO

CANONICAL COMMENTARY

CHAPTER IV

The Nature, Characteristics, and Object of the Obligation

ARTICLE I. THE NATURE OF THE OBLIGATION

In essence the obligation of the application of Mass for the people is this: those who have the care of souls are bound by an obligation in justice, founded in divine law, of applying the special fruit of the sacrifice of the Mass for the souls committed to their care. That such an obligation exists is evident from the fact that the Council of Trent says that it is commanded by a divine precept to every one to whom the care of souls is committed, to know his sheep, and to offer sacrifice for them.[1] Since this is an obligation derived ultimately from the divine law, it cannot be regarded as having had its origin with the council of Trent, but rather it must have been capable of being known by those bound, before its statement in the Canons of that Council.

The three papal documents on the subject of this obligation naturally treat of its nature. Pope Benedict XIV, in his encyclical letter, *Cum semper oblatas*,[2] emphasized the fact that the duty by which pastors of souls are bound to apply the Holy Sacrifice for souls committed to their care was declared by the Council of Trent to be an obligation originating in a divine precept. He further declared that the words of the Council themselves were clear and their meaning obvious, and that in addition the Sacred Congregation of the Council have constantly proclaimed

[1] Sess. XXIII, *de ref.*, c. I.

[2] Benedictus XIV, ep. encycl. *cum semper oblatas*, 19 aug., 1774—*Fontes*, n. 345.

that those to whom the care of souls had been entrusted were bound in virtue of this precept not only to celebrate Mass, but further to apply the special fruit of the Mass for the souls committed to them.

Pope Pius IX went further in his exposition of the nature of the obligation. It may be summarized as in the following. Christ instituted a priesthood identical with His own. The sacrifice which He offered, His priests offer. It is the sacrifice of reconciliation. The Pope then goes on to say, "Now as every high priest, taken from among men, is ordained for men in the things that pertain to God, to offer gifts and sacrifices for sins, it follows plainly, as you are well aware, that the Holy Sacrifice of the Mass should be applied by pastors for the souls committed to their care." [3]

Pope Leo continued the general theme of these papal documents by stating that conspicuous among the duties of those ministers of sacred things who have the care of souls is the duty of offering the Holy Sacrifice of the Mass expressly for the welfare of the people over whom they rule. He noted that the Fathers of Trent asserted this duty as one derived from a divine precept. Then he continued by pointing out that, speaking in broad and general terms, it is not difficult to perceive how closely the episcopal duty of offering for the people harmonizes with the sacred text and with the traditions of the past. For whatever passages furnish causes or motives demonstrating why pastors of souls should offer prayer and sacrifice for those under their care, also prove that this duty is peculiarly an episcopal one. The Pope referred to two texts from St. Paul's Epistles in which the apostle speaks of his praying and making supplication to God for the people to whom the Epistles were addressed.[4] From them the Pope deduced that in this supplication in which Paul says he persevered with joy, there was no doubt that the Eucharistic Sacrifice was included since, as Paul himself testified, it was for the sake of this chiefly that Christian high priests were instituted.[5]

---

[3] Pius IX, ep. encycl. *Amantissimi Redemptoris,* 3 maii, 1853—*Fontes,* n. 524, §4.

[4] Coloss. I, 9; Philip. I, 3–4.

[5] Leo XIII, litt. ap. *In suprema,* 10 iun., 1882—*Fontes,* n. 585.

From these papal documents dealing expressly with the nature of the obligation of the application of Mass for the people, one is warranted in making the following summary:

1. There is a certain obligation binding those with the care of souls to offer Mass for the people committed to their care.

2. This obligation was stated by the Council of Trent to be of divine precept.

3. The existence of the obligation by divine precept follows plainly from the words of St. Paul on the function of a high priest.

4. It may also be deduced from the fact that St. Paul offered prayer and supplication for his people.

To examine more closely the nature of this obligation it is necessary to consult its analysis by commentators. Many do not consider the question or merely mention it in passing. Vermeersch omits any mention of this particular point in both his Theologia Moralis and his Epitome Iuris Canonici.[6] Wernz-Vidal,[7] Aertnys-Damen,[8] Fanfani,[9] Woywod,[10] Herve,[11] Slater,[12] and Coronata[13] limit themselves to saying that the obligation is of divine law, and give as their reference the Council of Trent. Ferreres makes the statement that all pastors of souls are bound by natural and divine law to celebrate sometimes for their flock;

---

[6] *Theologia Moralis* (3 ed., 4 vols., Romae, 1933); Vermeersch-Creusen, *Epitome Iuris Canonici* (3 vols., Mechlinae, 1934-1937). (Hereafter this work will be cited as *Epitome.*)

[7] *Ius Canonicum* (7 Tom. in 8 vols., Romae, 1927-1938), II, 604. (Hereafter this work will be cited as *Ius Canonicum.*)

[8] *Theologia Moralis* (13 ed., 3 vols., Taurini: Marietti, 1939), I, n. 1145. (Hereafter this work will be cited as *Theologia Moralis.*)

[9] *De Iure Parochorum* (ed. altera, Taurini: Marietti, 1936), p. 240.

[10] *Homiletic and Pastoral Review,* XXI (1931), 747.

[11] *Manuale Theologiae Dogmaticae* (14 ed., 4 vols., Parisiis: Apud Berché et Pagis. 1936), IV, 143.

[12] Slater, "The Mass Pro Populo,"—*The Ecclesiastical Review,* LXII (1920), 634.

[13] *Institutiones Iuris Canonici* (ed. altera aucta et emendata, 5 vols., Taurini: Marietti, 1933-1939), I, n. 397, footnote 6. (Hereafter cited as *Institutiones.*)

and the reason assigned is that pastors ought to feed their sheep.[14]

Toso treats the question at greater length. He states that the root and foundation of the obligation consists in this, that a cleric freely and legitimately receives the spiritual care of a definite people as their own proper pastor; hence follows as the noblest part of the office which he has undertaken, the natural obligation in justice of praying for the flock entrusted to him, and hence of offering the Holy Sacrifice for them. For this offering is the principal parochial function. This natural obligation is enforced in the provisions of the common law under which there arises an obligation of applying the Mass for the people when these elements are present:

1. a people determined by a competent ecclesiastical authority;
2. a cleric legitimately designated by the same authority as the proper pastor of these people, for the actual necessary care of souls.

He notes that the people cannot be so determined except by a territorial division.[15]

Cappello analyzes the obligation and decides that it is:

of *divine-natural law,* inasmuch as there is a quasi-contract between the pastor and the people, from which there falls on the pastor by the very nature of the contract the obligation of being responsible for everything which is of benefit to the souls;

of *divine-positive law,* inasmuch as Christ wished and commanded that the Sacrifice of the Mass be offered by the pastor for the spiritual welfare of the people who have been committed to his care.[16]

More carefully expressed is the notion of Gasparri that the precept is imposed by divine law and that the basis of the precept is found in an examination of the office of pastor, or in the notion

---

[14] *Compendium Theologiae Moralis* (ed. 14, 2 vols., Barcinone: Subirana, 1928), II, n. 465. (Hereafter cited as *Compendium.*)

[15] Toso, *Commentaria Minora ad Codicem Juris Canonici* (5 vols., Romae: Marietti, 1924–1930), canon 466. (Hereafter cited as *Commentaria Minora.*)

[16] Cappello, *Tractatus Canonico-Moralis de Sacramentis* (3 ed., 3 vols. in 6, Taurini: Marietti, 1932–1939), I, n. 636. (Hereafter cited as *De Sacramentis.*)

of the care of souls, although it may also be piously believed that Christ " viva voce " and expressly issued it to the Apostles.[17]

Cocchi refers to Cappello and says that the obligation is of natural and divine law: natural—because there is a quasi-contract between the pastor and the people by which the pastor is bound to be responsible for everything which is required for the salvation of souls; divine—for the Tridentine Fathers repeated that this obligation has its source in divine law according to the words of St. Paul.[18]

Tarquinius, in his opinion as a consultor, preliminary to a response of the Sacred Congregation of the Council, treated the question explicitly. He was seeking the basis in positive divine law on which this precept of applying Mass for the people rests. He decided that the precept cannot otherwise be deduced than " from the nature and notion of the pastoral office." He too used the phrase employed in Gasparri, " ex indole et notione officii pastoralis." He concluded that the pastoral office in its entirety, or plenitude, bears with it by its very nature the duty of offering sacrifice for the people.[19]

Prümmer also treats the question explicitly, and after mentioning the text from St. Paul's Epistle to the Hebrews, and the words of the Council of Trent, he decides that the natural law itself prescribes that the pastor of souls, in virtue of a contract undertaken and an office received, ought to foster and procure the spiritual welfare of his flock with all his powers. But this seems impossible unless the faithful repeatedly assist at the Sacrifice of the Mass, and receive not only the general, but also the ministerial fruits of the Mass. Therefore, the pastor of souls in virtue of the nature of his office, is bound to say the Mass

---

[17] Gasparri, *De Sanctissima Eucharistia,* I, n. 496: "Putamus igitur hoc praeceptum descendere ex indole et notione officii pastoralis, ita ut sufficiat, prouti eruitur etiam ex verbis S. Pauli, ut quis pontifex sit, ut intelligatur constitutus ad sacrificia pro populi peccatis offerenda."

[18] Cocchi, *Commentarium in Codicem Iuris Canonici* (3 ed., 8 vols., Taurini: Marietti, 1931–1940), n. 261. (Hereafter cited as *Commentarium.*)

[19] *ASS,* I, 391: ". . . non aliunde repeti censebat, quam ex indole et notione officii pastoralis. Sufficit enim prout eruitur etiam ex Pauli verbis, ut quis pontifex sit, ut intelligatur constitutus ad sacrificia pro populi peccatis offerenda."

sometimes for the people committed to his care.[20] Kaiser says the obligation is special, not in virtue of orders or of revenues, but of the pastoral office and of the quasi-contract in justice made by the pastor when assuming the *cura animarum*.[21] Sipos quotes Tarquinius and adds that the obligation has its source in justice, and that they, who are the proper pastors of a definite flock, are bound to it under a quasi-contract.[22]

For the most part, then, the commentators do not consider at any length the question of the nature of the obligation incumbent on those with care of souls. Those who do treat the matter base the obligation on two grounds:

1. by reason of the quasi-contract existing between the people and the one to whom the care of souls is committed (Cappello, Noldin, Sipos, Prümmer, Kaiser, Cocchi).

2. from the very notion and nature of the pastoral office (Gasparri, Tarquinius, Prümmer, and in different terms, Toso).

The idea of an obligation based on a quasi-contract seems to be the generally accepted notion. Yet its proponents do not state expressly in just what this quasi-contract consists. Presumably it amounts to this, that the people are bound by an obligation to provide for the support of the pastor, or more accurately for the support of that person to whom the care of souls is given. He, in return, is bound to provide for the spiritual welfare of those souls committed to his care, and among the means necessary for this is the application of the Mass for the people. Yet the idea of a quasi-contract as stated in these terms cannot be upheld. It is not because the people possess a right as a *quid pro quo* to application of the Mass that the obligation exists. It is unanimously admitted now that whether or not the one holding the office receives a salary or a return from that office, so long as he retains the care of souls he retains the obligation of applying

---

[20] Prümmer, *Manuale Theologiae Moralis* (8 ed., 3 vols., Friburgi-Brisgoviae: Herder, 1936), III, n. 255. (Hereafter cited as *Theologia Moralis.*)

[21] Kaiser, "Ecclesiastical Legislation on the Missa Pro Populo,"—*ER,* LXI (1919), 364.

[22] Sipos, *Enchiridion Iuris Canonici* (3 ed., Pecs 1936), p. 260.

for the people.[23] Since this is so it cannot be said that there is a bilateral contract. An acceptable notion is the idea of an obligation based on a unilateral contract, binding not under strict commutative justice but by a grave obligation of the natural law, in this case based on legal justice, or the duty of an official to the spiritual society.

Cappello's statement that the obligation is of positive divine law inasmuch as Christ wished and commanded that the Sacrifice of the Mass be offered for the spiritual salvation of their flock by those to whom the care of the people has been committed, is an assumption of what needs to be proved. There is available no text of the words of Christ commanding specifically the application of the Mass for the people. Gasparri states more properly that this is something that may be piously believed.

A more acceptable basis for the obligation under divine precept is given by those who hold that it arises from the very notion and nature of the pastoral office, from the office to which is attached the care of souls. In the observations contained in the *Acta Apostolicae Sedis,* preliminary to a response of the Sacred Congregation of the Council, one reads the very definite and unequivocal statement, that one thing is required and suffices for imposing the obligation, that is, that any one be the proper pastor of a determined flock, so that the care of souls, in the strict sense, is committed to him.[24]

This idea that the root of the obligation is founded in the possession of an office to which the care of souls is attached, may be developed further. By his ordination to the priesthood, a priest is set apart to offer sacrifice to God on behalf of the people. This is true of every priest. When a priest says Mass, all the faithful receive some spiritual benefit from it, a share in the general fruit of the Mass. But, in addition to that, from the fact that he is placed in charge of souls for their eternal welfare, the pastor of souls has certain definite and grave obligations. He is responsible to God for the exercise of his prerogative in the interests of a definite group of Christians, to aid them in discharging

---

[23] Benedictus XIV, ep. encycl. *Cum semper oblatas,* 19 aug., 1774—*Fontes,* n. 345; C. 339, §1.

[24] S. C. C., *Wratislavien.,* 13 iul., 1918—*AAS,* XI (1919), 46.

their spiritual obligations.[25] He must feed his sheep, and his sheep are those souls committed to his care. Chief among the means which have been committed to him for the salvation of souls is mediation through Sacrifice of the Mass. To aid the definite group committed to his care, to be the true "pastor" he is bound to apply the Mass for the people.

The obligation, then, is based upon, and has its roots in, the office of caring for souls. That office is the immediate root of the obligation. That office is of divine law.

But the obligation of applying Mass for the people is binding on bishops by a duty prior to that of parish priests, for the obligation of parish priests arises from that divine law which is called *mediate* and *hypothetical*. To bishops, on the contrary, belongs the pastoral office directly inasmuch as the Holy Ghost placed them to rule the Church of God and it belongs to them also primarily because the full and entire care of souls is in their hands, and only a part of this ministry is entrusted to parish priests, that part, namely, which is assigned them by the Church.[26]

It is important to note that the obligation is based not on orders alone. A titular bishop is not bound to this obligation because he has neither the use nor the exercise of that jurisdictional power received in episcopal consecration. The pastoral office in its fullness resides in the bishops by divine law. But, by the fact of consecration, a bishop does not possess by divine law the use and exercise of the pastoral office.[27] The one root of the obligation is the care of souls, entrusted to the bishop by the Pope, entrusted normally to the parish priest by the bishop.

ARTICLE II. CHARACTERISTICS OF THE OBLIGATION

The ecclesiastical determination of this divine obligation has

---

[25] Meier, *Penal Administrative Procedure Against Negligent Pastors* (The Catholic University of America Canon Law Studies, No. 140, Washington, D. C.: The Catholic University of America, 1940), p. 1.

[26] Leo XIII, litt. ap. *In suprema*, 10 iun., 1882—*Fontes*, n. 585.

[27] Hervé (*Manuale Dogmatice Theologicae*, IV, n. 143) seems to differ: "Decet, tamen, ex caritate, ut aliquando . . . Missam applicent ovibus suis, episcopi titulares (c. 348,2), item praelati regulares, *qui veram habent curam animarum*."

resulted in a description of the obligation as *real, personal, local,* and *affixed to a definite day*.

(a) It is considered a *real* obligation because it exists until satisfied, and it does not cease with the passage of that day on which the law required the Mass to be offered, even though it was omitted in good faith or for a legitimate excuse.

(b) It is considered a *personal* obligation because the person on whom the obligation rests must offer the Mass himself unless prevented by a legitimate impediment or excused for a just cause. Prümmer declares that the reason is that the Sacrifice of the Cross was offered by Christ the Pastor of all, and so it is most fitting that a pastor, taking the place of Christ the Pastor, should himself apply the fruits of the Sacrifice for his subjects.[28] Ferreres' explanation of this obligation of the person is this: prayers and sacrifices which we ourselves offer for ourselves or for those specially joined to us by blood, subordination or obedience, are more efficacious than if we offer them for strangers or through strangers. Further, the faithful profit more when present at Mass applied for themselves than when present at Mass which is not applied for them.[29] De Meester says that the reason for the personal nature of the obligation seems to be that although the Sacrifice is fruitful *ex opere operato,* the fruit of the Sacrifice can be greater *ex opere operantis,* and in the law it is thought that the prayers for the flock of him whose sheep these are will be more efficacious in God's sight than the prayers of him who, relative to the flock, is merely a *mercenarius*. Hence in the celebration of Mass for the people the pastor exercises the ministry of a specially commissioned mediator who, therefore, is not to pass his commission on to another.[30]

These statements are not conclusive arguments so much as attempts to set forth the fact that a personal obligation harmonizes best with the pastoral office and so to justify a characteristic which is so evident in pertinent ecclesiastical legislation.

---

[28] *Theologia Moralis,* III, n. 258, b.

[29] Ferreres, *Compendium,* II, n. 470.

[30] De Meester, *Juris Canonici et Juris Canonico-Civilis Compendium* (nova ed., 3 vols. in 4, Brugis: Desclee, De Brouwer, 1921–1928), n. 846. (Hereafter this work will be cited as *Compendium.*)

(c) It is considered as a local obligation because the Mass for the people must be celebrated in the parish church unless circumstances demand or counsel otherwise. The local obligation binds only the parish priest and those who are juridically regarded as such.

(d) It is a temporal obligation because its fulfillment is fixed to a definite day, that is, the Mass in each instance is to be offered on the day assigned and is not to be postponed or advanced unless there is a just cause or a sufficient reason for so doing.

ARTICLE III. THE OBJECT OF THE OBLIGATION

A minor question that some few authors treat is the object of the obligation, that is, " for whom is the Mass for the people to be applied?" Does the term "pro populo" include the deceased as well as the living? The Code indicates the object as "pro populo sibi commisso," but this description as well as that used in the Council of Trent, "cum divino praecepto mandatum sit omnibus, quibus animarum cura commissa est . . . pro his sacrificium offerre" makes it clear that the mind of the Church is that only the living are to be regarded as the object of the obligation to apply Mass for the people. The souls of the dead cannot be said to be committed to the care of pastors or bishops. This is the prevailing and the more correct opinion.[31] Some few authors hold that there is an obligation to apply the Mass also for the deceased members of the flock.[32] The author of an article in *L'Ami du Clerge* feels bound to agree with Noldin that there is not an obligation of including the dead in the application of the Mass for the people, since strict reason says that the dead are subject to the power of God alone and are no longer parishioners of any one. He does incline to Berardi's view for "moral reasons," e.g. the

[31] De Meester, *Compendium*, II, n. 844; Cappello, *De Sacramentis*, I, n. 637; Kaiser, "Ecclesiastical Legislation on the Missa Pro Populo."—*ER*, LXI (1919), 363; Woywod, *HPR*, XXI (1921), 553; Noldin, *De Sacramentis*, n. 183, d; Koudelka, *Pastors, Their Rights and Duties*, p. 53; *L'Ami du Clerge* (1909), 719.

[32] Buvee, *Memento Pratique De Ministere Paroissial* (Parisiis, 1921), p. 35; Berardi, *De Parocho Compendium*, n. 76; Mahoney, *Clergy Review*, III (1932), 408.

pastor ought not to abandon his parishioners after their death; the dead do have juridical rights even in the Code such as the right to Christian burial and to prayers.

Mahoney objects to the view that there is an obligation to apply only for the living, on the grounds that this solution is based on a purely legalistic interpretation of texts. He says that, while the dead are not parishioners strictly speaking, they have been parishioners and the priest will surely not be directed by the Church to abandon them when dead. Further nothing in the phrase of the Council of Trent proves that the words "pro his" refer only to the living, and from the point of view of a contracted obligation of justice, there can be no doubt that benefactions of the dead have largely contributed to the permanent support of the priest.

These arguments of Mahoney are not valid. The question is, what is the canonical obligation of the priest who is bound to the Mass for the people? The reasons adduced to prove the obligation of including the dead in his intention merely show how fitting it is to pray for deceased parishioners; they do not show any obligation under either divine or ecclesiastical law to include them in the application of Mass for the people. Further in directing the priest to apply the Mass for the people under his care, i.e., the living, the Church can hardly be said to direct him to abandon the dead. The fact that the offerings once given by those now dead did contribute to the support of the priest, does not constitute a proof that, by the words "pro populo" the Code means "the people committed to you, even those now dead." Since it is not the offerings of the faithful which oblige the pastor to apply Mass for the people of his parish that argument has no validity in proving an obligation on the pastor to apply Mass for the deceased members of his parish.[33]

Noldin [34] and Cappello [35] agree that any mention of the dead or

---

[33] *Supra*, p. 50.

[34] *De Sacramentis*, n. 183, 1 d.

[35] "Decet tamen ut conditionate intentio extendatur etiam ad defunctos. Dicimus conditionate, quatenus id fieri queat sine praejudicio vivorum, qui ad integrum fructum sacrificii ministerialem ius habent ex mente Ecclesiae." —Cappello, *De Sacramentis*, I, n. 637.

any remembrance of them in the Mass applied for the people must be made conditionally, i.e., inasmuch as it can be done without injuring the rights of the living, since the living parishioners have a right to the whole ministerial fruit of the sacrifice. But since they admit that the living parishioners have a right to the whole fruit why should there be any mention of the dead? How would an application of the Mass for the people to the dead under the condition that there be no injury to the rights of the living be of any benefit to the dead? Once having established the principle that there is no obligation to offer for the dead in offering the Mass for the people, and also the principle that the living have a right in justice to the whole fruit of that Mass, why insert an unnecessary and unavailing condition?

ARTICLE IV. THE MORAL ASPECT OF THE OBLIGATION

While it is not strictly a matter of Canon Law, the question of the gravity of the obligation of offering the Mass for the people has some place in any extensive treatment of the subject. Every author who treats the topic, without an exception, agrees that the deliberate omission of even one Mass for the people is a mortal sin.[36] It is regarded by them as a sin against justice, entailing the obligation of saying the Mass either personally or through someone else. It is a grave sin *ex toto genere suo,* admitting no parvity of matter.

The secondary obligations, based on the time, the place, the personal celebration, do not seem to share the same gravity. Whereas there is no excusing cause for the real obligation, since the Mass must always be applied unless a dispensation is obtained, the law of the Church does permit excusing causes with regard to these secondary characteristics of celebrant, and of time and place of celebration. Therefore so far as the questions of single omissions of these secondary obligations are concerned,

---

[36] "Theologians seem to agree at least that the real obligation of the Missa pro populo . . . is a grave one. Their conclusion is based chiefly upon the nature and purpose of the pastoral office in which the celebration of the Mass constitutes the great central means for promoting the spiritual welfare of the flock."—Kaiser, "Ecclesiastical Legislation on the Missa Pro Populo."—*ER,* LXI (1919), 426.

there is no doubt that such omissions, even without a reason, are at most venial sins. It is true that both Vermeersch and De Meester hold that to celebrate personally, on the day decreed, and in the parish church, is of grave obligation, grave *ex genere suo*.[37] However, since an obligation which is grave *ex genere suo* admits of parvity of matter, their opinion, in effect, says that a single omission of these secondary obligations, or one at rare intervals, would be only a venial sin, even if there were no excusing cause.

A question of greater weight is that concerning the gravity of frequent violations of the secondary obligations. What is to be thought of the gravity of the sin of a pastor who habitually anticipates or postpones the obligation, or who at the beginning of a year transfers the obligation of the Mass for the people to his curate, or to a missionary? There is agreement among authors regarding the fact that it is a grave sin, without just cause, *frequently* to have the Mass said by a substitute, or to say it elsewhere than in the parish church, or to apply it on another day than that decreed in the law. This is the opinion of Lehmkuhl,[38] Noldin,[39] Davis,[40] Arregui,[41] Herve,[42] Ferreres,[43] Leroux,[44]

---

37 ". . . ad ulteriores determinationes nempe ut celebret per se, die statuto et in ecclesia parochiali teneri parochum ex virtute obedientiae obligatione grave ex genere suo."—De Meester, *Compendium*, n. 849.

". . . aliae determinationes obligant sub gravi per se, sed levitatem materiae admittunt."—Vermeersch, *Epitome*, I, n. 553.

38 *Theologiae Moralis* (11 ed., 2 vols., Friburgi Brisgoviae, 1910), II, n. 196.

39 "Eorum ergo omissione peccatum grave non committitur, nisi *saepe et fere ex consuetudine* violentur."—Noldin, *De Sacramentis*, n. 183.

40 "It is also a grave sin, without just cause, frequently to have the Mass said by a substitute, or not to say it in the parish church."—Davis, *Moral and Pastoral Theology*, IV, 108.

41 *Summarium Theologiae Moralis* (ed. 13, Romae: Typis Pont. Universitatis Gregorianae. 1937), p. 373.

42 *Manuale Theologiae Dogmaticae*, IV, n. 143, 2°.

43 *Compendium*, II, n. 471.

44 Leroux, "La Messe 'Pro Populo'"—*Revue Ecclesiastique de Liege*, XIV (1922–1923), pp. 148–157.

Veermeersch,[45] De Meester,[46] and Koudelka.[47] The weight of authority of these authors, in addition to the fact that their opinion seems without opposition from other commentators, makes this opinion practically certain.

From what has been said it follows that the duty of the application of the Mass for the people, viewed in itself, binds under grave sin. A single deliberate omission, not a mere postponement, of the Mass would be a grave sin. As regards the restrictions of person, time and place the obligation binds only under venial sin, unless the neglect implies contempt of the law, or the omission be frequent or habitual, or the fulfillment of the obligation be unduly delayed. St. Alphonsus considers a delay of two months as constituting grave matter.[48]

---

[45] *Epitome*, I, n. 553.

[46] *Compendium*, II, n. 849.

[47] "For a grave sin frequent violations of the temporal, local and personal aspects of this duty are required."—Koudelka, *Pastors, Their Rights and Duties* (The Catholic University of America Canon Law Studies, n. 11, Washington, D. C.: The Catholic University of America, 1921), p. 51.

[48] St. Alphonsus Liguori, *Theologia Moralis,* VI, 326.

CHAPTER V

The Subjects of the Obligation

ARTICLE I. THE SUBJECTS OF THE OBLIGATION IN GENERAL

The obligation of applying the Mass for the people binds all who have the care of souls. The specific consideration of those who are subject to it calls for certain convenient divisions based on their office in order to clear the ground for this consideration. But first it is necessary to speak of the exemption of some who might seem from their positions to incur this obligation but actually do not do so.

A. Clerics Not Bound by the Obligation

1. *Titular bishops.* They have no obligation, although it is fitting in charity that they should sometimes apply Mass for the inhabitants of their titular Sees.[1] The canon uses the word "aliquando." Cappello and Herve alone among the commentators give it definiteness. They assume that it means eight or ten times a year.[2] The canon is in accord with the mind and the legislation of Pope Leo XIII, who felt that, taking equity and episcopal charity into account, it could not but seem proper that they should occasionally offer the Holy Sacrifice to implore God to look down with mercy upon the wretched condition of those churches the name and title of which they bear.[3]

2. *Auxiliary and Coadjutor Bishops.* A coadjutor given to a bishop incapable of performing his episcopal duties has all the rights and duties of a bishop.[4] This does not, however, accord-

---

[1] C. 348, §2.

[2] Cappello, *De Sacramentis,* I, n. 638, §3; Herve, *Manuale Theologiae Dogmaticae,* IV, n. 143, 1º b.

[3] Leo XIII, litt. ap., *In suprema,* 10 iun. 1882—*Fontes,* n. 585.

[4] C. 351, §2.

ing to the authors, include the application of the Mass for the people.[5]

3. *Religious Superiors.* It is quite evident that religious superiors are not bound by the ecclesiastical law of applying Mass for the people. The law is silent on the matter, and the author has not found a single writer who maintains that there is such an ecclesiastical obligation. But there is a difference of opinion regarding the obligation of these superiors under the divine law. Prümmer,[6] Wernz-Vidal,[7] and Lehmkuhl[8] hold that religious superiors are bound by an obligation of the divine law of applying Mass for their subjects. Genicot,[9] Noldin,[10] Herve,[11] Vermeersch,[12] Marc-Gestermann,[13] and Leroux[14] hold that there is no obligation resting on them but that it is fitting in charity that they should sometimes apply mass for their subjects. The ma-

---

[5] Wernz-Vidal, *Ius Canonicum,* II, n. 619; Merkelbach, *Summa Theologiae Moralis,* III. n. 368; Cappello, *De Sacramentis,* I, n. 638, 2, a.

[6] ". . . haud dubium videtur, quin ex jure divino teneantur ad applicandam Missam aliquoties pro subditis."—Prümmer, *Theologia Moralis,* III, n. 254.

[7] ". . . non soluti sunt a praecepto divino pro ovibus sibi commissis saltem aliquoties durante officio offerendi sacrificium Missae."—*Ius Canonicum,* IV, n. 76, a.

[8] Lehmkuhl, *Theologia Moralis,* II, n. 266.

[9] "Superiores religiosi certe non comprehenduntur legibus quas Ecclesia de hoc argumento tulit. Practice autem maxime decet ut interdum pro subditis litent."—Genicot, *Institutiones Theologiae Moralis,* II, n. 197, 3°. (Hereafter cited as *Institutiones.*)

[10] "Quamvis praelati regulares missae sacrificium pro subditis suis applicare stricto jure non teneantur, quia tamen cura pastoralis in subditos suos ab ecclesia vere eis commissa sit, summopere convenit ut et ipsi missae sacrificium pro subditis suis offerant."—Noldin, *De Sacramentis,* n. 183, c.

[11] "Non tenentur praelati regulares. Decet tamen ex caritate . . ."—*Manuale Theologiae Dogmaticae,* IV, n. 143.

[12] "De stricta tamen obligatione Superiorum regularium non constat."—Vermeersch, *Theologia Moralis,* III, n. 265.

[13] "Praelati regulares non tenentur qualibet dominica pro suis subditis applicare. Nihilominus, cum ipsis specialis cura pastoralis ab ecclesia sit commissa, jure meritoque decet ut aliquoties pro suis orent et sacrificent."—Marc-Gestermann, *Institutiones Morales,* II, n. 1606.

[14] Leroux, "La Messe 'Pro Populo'"—*Revue Ecclésiastique de Liége,* XIV (1922–1923), 148–157.

jority of those who consider this question seem to feel that the obligation of the divine law cannot be proved. Kaiser, however, insists that for all regular superiors the obligation seems to hold, that is, they are probably bound from a divine precept at least hypothetical, since they have external jurisdiction and therefore have a greater share of the pastoral office of the parish priest. This obligation, he feels, is even more certain for superiors of congregations exempted from parochial jurisdiction.[15] The more correct opinion would seem to be that which holds that religious superiors are bound by the divine law sometimes to apply the sacrifice of the Mass for their subjects. There can be no question as to the non-existence of an obligation under the law of the Code. But since the obligation in divine law is so clearly stated in the Council of Trent for all who have responsibility for souls and since there is no doubt that religious superiors have the care of souls the presumption would seem to be that they also are bound and any exception in their case from the obligation stated in the Council of Trent would have to be proved.

4. *Adjutants* (*vicarii adjutores*). Adjutants are those who have been deputed by the local ordinary to assume the duties of a pastor who, due to some permanent impediment, for example, old age, mental debility, blindness, is not able satisfactorily to conduct the affairs of the parish or discharge the corresponding obligations. If they take the place of the pastor in all things they have all the rights and obligations of the pastor, but the canon expressly exempts the application of Mass for the people and explicitly determines that this obligation remains with the pastor.[16]

5. *Vicars substitute* (*vicarii substituti*), i.e., they who have been legitimately constituted to perform the parochial duties, either because the pastor is to be absent for a period exceeding a week, because he has been compelled to leave suddenly or because, having been deprived of his parish, he is appealing his case to the Holy See.[17] Such substitutes take the place of the pastor in all

---

[15] Kaiser, "Ecclesiastical Legislation on the 'Missa Pro Populo,'" *ER*, LXI (1919), 368.

[16] C. 475, §2.

[17] Canons 474; 465, §§4 & 5; 1923, §2.

that pertains to the care of souls.[18] However, an exception is made for those duties which the pastor can and chooses to discharge personally even during his absence, notably the offering of Mass for the people.[19] Kaiser says that the reason for this exception is that the canon does not give temporary substitutes full parochial rights and duties; hence they need not assume the obligation of the Mass for the people, unless the Ordinary or the pastor so designates.[20] His conclusion, of course, is correct. But the canon very definitely gives full rights and duties to the substitute, unless the Ordinary or the pastor restricts him.[21] If the Ordinary or the pastor places no exception the substitute is bound to assume all the duties of the pastor. The only reason why he is not bound to the application of the Mass for the people is the personal nature of the obligation, which remains the pastor's unless, in legitimate absence, the latter wishes to take advantage of the privilege granted him by can. 466, §5 of satisfying his obligation through the priest who takes his place in the parish. Therefore, contrary to Kaiser, the fact that the vicar substitute is not bound to the Mass for the people is not based on a limitation or defect in the powers granted him in the canon, but in the nature of the obligation of the Mass for the people.

6. *Chaplains*. They are not bound. The Code does not list the application of the Mass for the people among their duties. A pre-Code response declared that they were not bound since they were not pastors.[22] This principle is even more certain under the new law.[23] The status of military chaplains depends on the par-

[18] C. 474.

[19] Ayrinhac, *Constitution of the Church* (New York, 1930: Longmans-Green), n. 297, 2º.

[20] Kaiser, "Ecclesiastical Legislation on the 'Missa Pro Populo,'" *ER*, LXI (1919), p. 368.

[21] "Vicarius substitutus qui constituitur ad normam can. 465, §4, §5, et can. 1923, §2, locum parochi tenet *in omnibus quae ad curam animarum spectant,* nisi Ordinarius loci vel parochus aliquid exceperint."—C. 474.

[22] S. C. C. Nullius Clunier, 22 maii, 1909—*AAS,* I (1909), 546.

[23] "At ab illa obligatione immunes sunt . . . capellani, omnium illorum institutorum, v. g. hospitalium, collegiorum, quae in veras parochias non sunt erecta."—Wernz-Vidal, *Ius Canonicum,* IV, n. 76, a; cf. also Cappello, *De Sacramentis,* I, n. 641; Herve, *Manuale Dogmaticae Theologiae,* IV, n. 143, 1, b.

ticular laws of the Holy See.[24] Chaplains in the armed forces of the United States have no obligation to say the *Missa pro populo* but it is commendable that sometimes they so apply the Mass out of charity.[25]

B. Clerics Bound by the Obligation

Specifically the following are the subjects of the obligation:

1. *The Pope.* The Council of Trent stated that it is commanded by divine precept that all to whom the care of souls is committed should offer Mass for their flock. To the Pope is given the care of all the souls in the whole world, in every diocese and in every parish church.[26] Therefore the Roman Pontiff, solely from the obligation of the divine law, without being in any way bound by the ecclesiastical law, is obliged sometimes during the year to offer Mass for the people committed to his care, namely all the faithful.[27] The Pope is bound by this obligation from the moment in which he takes possession of his office, that is, from the moment he accepts the election.[28]

2. *Residential bishops.* After they have taken possession of their See, and despite any excuse based on a small revenue or any other exception, they are obliged to offer Mass for the people committed to them, on all Sundays, holy days, and even suppressed feasts.[29] Genicot notes that they have taken possession

---

[24] "Circa militum capellanos sive majores sive minores standum peculiaribus Sanctae Sedis praescriptis."—C. 451, §3.

[25] Appendix, *Regulae A Cappelanis Castrensibus Observandae,* n. 12, "Applicandae Missae pro populo obligatione non tenentur Cappellani Castrenses. Nihilominus eos in Domino hortamur ut eandem pro suis subditis aliquando ex caritate applicent." (Resp. S. C. de Sacr. ad Ex'mum ac R'mum Delegatum Apostolicum; cf. Litt. Ex'mi ac R'mi Delegati Apostolici ad Ex'mum ac R'mum Vicarium Castrensen, die 31 Maii 1941, Prot. num. 59/40.)—*Facultates Castrenses,* p. 16.

[26] C. 218, §2.

[27] Cappello, *De Sacramentis,* I, n. 638; Prümmer, *Theologia Moralis,* III, n. 254; Gasparri, *De Eucharistia,* I, n. 497; Davis, *Moral Theology,* III, 106.

[28] ". . . illa obligatio celebrandi et applicandi Missam urget omnes pastores animarum a momento suscepti muneris pastoralis, i. e., in Romano Pontifice ab electione accepta."—Wernz-Vidal, *Ius Canonicum,* IV, n. 76.

[29] C. 339, §1.

of their See when they have presented their Apostolic Bulls to the Chapter.[30]

3. *Cardinals of the suburbican Sees.* They are true bishops of their dioceses and enjoy in them the same power which a residential bishop obtains in his own diocese.[31]

4. *Abbots or Prelates Nullius.* These are prelates who preside over a territory of their own, inhabited by clergy and people subject to no other diocesan authority. They are called Abbots or Prelates *Nullius,* viz., of no diocese according as their church is abbatial or simply prelatial.[32] They have the same ordinary powers and the same obligations enforceable with the sanctions, as attach to residential bishops in their own dioceses.[33]

5. *Vicars and Prefects Apostolic.* They are vicars of the Apostolic See, with episcopal jurisdiction, appointed for regions where a full diocesan organization cannot as yet be established or restored.[34] They must apply Mass for their subjects at least on the feasts of Christmas, Epiphany, Easter, Ascension, Pentecost, Corpus Christi, the Immaculate Conception, the Assumption of the Blessed Virgin, SS. Peter and Paul, and All Saints, with due regard for the rules laid down in canon 339, §2 ff.[35] This is a new obligation, one which did not exist before the Code. Previously Vicars and Prefects Apostolic were not bound by an obligation of this kind in justice, or even in charity.[36] Toso once held the opposite view. Treating canon 306 at some length, he

[30] "Pro his omnibus incipit ista obligatio a momento quo possessionem sumunt muneris cui animarum cura annexa est, ex. gr. pro Episcopo a momento quo Bullas Apostolicas Capitulo exhibet."—Genicot, *Institutiones,* II, 197.

[31] C. 240, §1; Cappello, *De Sacramentis,* I, n. 638, 1, 2º.

[32] C. 319, §1.

[33] C. 323, 1; "Hinc-b)quoad obligationes, tenentur ad residentiam sicut Episcopi; ad applicationem Missae pro populo diebus quibus Episcopi tenentur."—Cocchi, *Commentarium,* III, n. 239.

[34] C. 293.

[35] C. 306.

[36] S. C. de prop. Fide, aug. 5, 1860—*Collectanea, S. C. P. F.* I, n. 1199; cf. S. C. de prop. Fide, aug. 18, 1866: "Ad 2 vitandam esse locutionem teneri ex charitate, dicendum vero esse *decere* ex charitate, idque ita ut nulla proprie dicta obligationis significatio appareat."—*Collectanea, S. C. P. F.* I, n. 1296.

argued that this obligation for Vicars and Prefects Apostolic does not bind in justice, or even in charity. His reasoning is that Vicars and Prefects Apostolic are not to be included among residential bishops; for there is only one Pastor who rules missionary regions in his own name and authority, namely the Roman Pontiff. Others, whether they are Vicars or quasi-pastors, have the office not in title but only in administration. Hence the pre-Code response that they were not bound in justice or charity. Hence, too, that decision still holds after the Code.

But what does Toso answer to canon 306 with its application to Vicars and Prefects Apostolic of canon 339, §2 and following? First he admits that there is no doubt that Vicars and Prefects Apostolic, on the eleven days taxatively enumerated in the canon are subject to an obligation of applying the Mass for the people committed to their care. But since this obligation cannot arise from justice, for through the Code no change is made in the juridic condition of these prelates, it remains that the matter of the new law establishes an obligation binding at the most in charity.

However, in his commentary on canon 466 Toso notes the fact that quasi-pastors are treated in the Code as are pastors and therefore they are bound in justice to apply the Mass for their subjects. This, he says, is a new obligation in the law. For before the Code *Praesules missionum* and missionaries themselves were not under any such obligation. But he notes that the Code, on the contrary, in Canon 466 uses the words, "obligatione tenetur," and in canon 306, "applicare debent." Hence in contrast to what he has thought elsewhere, he admits that not only quasi-pastors but also Vicars and Prefects Apostolic are bound in justice to apply Mass for their subjects.[37]

6. *Apostolic Administrators, Permanently Constituted.* They are prelates appointed by the Sovereign Pontiff, for special and grave reasons, to rule in his name a canonically erected diocese. They are bound by the same obligations as residential bishops.[38]

[37] ". . . Ex adverso Codex ait: obligatione tenetur; et can. 306: applicare debent: idest, secus ac alias existimavimus, ex justitia."—Toso, *Commentaria Minora*, C. 306 and 466.

[38] C. 315, §1.

Hence they are bound to apply Mass for their subjects on the same days as are residential bishops.[39]

7. *Vicars Capitular.* In the case of a vacancy in the episcopal See, the cathedral chapter, within eight days from the date the notice of vacancy was received, must appoint a vicar capitular, who will govern the diocese in the place of the chapter. He is bound to the obligation of applying Mass for the people according to the norm of canon 339.[40] This is an obligation which did not bind Vicars Capitular before the Code.[41]

8. *Pastors.* Priests to whom a parish is entrusted in title with the care of souls to be exercised under the authority of the Ordinary of the place are called pastors (*parochi*).[42] They are bound to apply Mass for the people according to the norm of canon 339.[43] It is important to note that a decree of erection, though it is the usual way of erecting a parish, is not necessary for validity. The letter of the Sacred Consistorial Congregation, issued before the Code, shows that the canonical erection of a parish may appear from several other essential elements that characterize a parish, namely, a certain defined territory, a definite population, a certain rector having the care of souls, and finally the authority of the bishop maintaining and approving this juridical condition.[44] Therefore if such parishes were certainly regarded before the Code as being canonically erected, this juridical condition is not changed by the Code. Hence rectors of such parishes which have in the past been constituted *de facto,* that is, enjoying the qualities indicated above but without any decree of canonical erection, even though their revenues consist only in voluntary offerings made by the faithful, are bound to apply the Mass for the people as true pastors.[45] The pastors of national parishes which have

---

[39] Coronata, *Institutiones,* I, n. 382, 2°, a; Vermeersch, *Epitome,* I, n. 433.

[40] C. 440.

[41] Chelodi, *Jus de Personis,* n. 218, footnote 1; Coronata, *Institutiones,* I, n. 461, 7°.

[42] C. 451, §1.

[43] C. 466, §1.

[44] S. C. Consist., 18 martii 1881—*Collectanea, S. C. P. F.,* II, n. 1584.

[45] S. C. C., *Principis Alberten. et Saskatoonen.,* 5 martii, 1932—*AAS,* XXV, 436; Bouscaren, *Canon Law Digest,* I, 151–154.

all the requirements of a canonical parish are, of course, also bound to the obligation. Usually national parishes are assigned a definite territory. Though it is often more extensive than that of a territorial parish, it is none the less clearly determined. Some national parishes may be strictly personal. If any national parish founded before the Code had no territorial limits but was actually strictly personal, it continues in this status after the Code. Yet even these seem to be recognized as canonical parishes.[46] Hence it can be concluded that the pastors of even personal national parishes have the obligation to apply Mass for the people.

9. *Quasi-pastors.* To pastors are assimilated by law in regard to parochial rights and obligations, as described in Canons 461, 463, 464, 470, the quasi-pastors or rectors of quasi-parishes erected in Vicariates or Prefectures Apostolic in accordance with the prescriptions of canon 216.[47] They are, therefore, bound by the obligation of offering Mass for the people according to the norms of canon 306.[48]

10. *Perpetual Vicars,* i.e., a vicar who is the actual parish priest of a parish united *pleno iure* to a religious community, a chapter church or some other moral person. To such a vicar pertains exclusively the complete care of souls with all the rights and obligations of a pastor according to the norms of the common law and according to approved diocesan statutes or laudable customs.[49] Saving laudable customs or diocesan statutes, they differ from other pastors only in name.[50] Hence, among the obligations of pastors to which these vicars are bound is the Mass for the people.[51] There are perpetual vicars of another type, that is, vicars in charge of filial churches, who are bound by this obligation. They are those whose churches, although they are not yet

46 C. 216, §4.

47 C. 451, §2, 1º.

48 C. 466, §1.

49 C. 471, §4.

50 Wernz-Vidal, *Ius Canonicum,* II, n. 740, III.

51 ". . . habent quoad residentiam et Missam pro populo easdem ac parochi obligationes."—Cocchi, *Commentarium,* III, n. 357, §4;

"Tenentur vicarii actuales qui actu paroeciam regunt, quando cura habitualis est penes personam moralem."—Cappello, *De Sacramentis,* I, n. 638, 9º.

erected into parishes, have nevertheless their own separate territory, and are entirely separated from and independent of the mother church. These vicars are bound to the obligation of Mass for the people if they are endowed with full parochial powers.[52]

11. *Administrators* (*vicarii oeconomi*) of vacant parishes. They enjoy the same rights and are bound by the same duties as pastors in those things which pertain to the care of souls.[53] Hence they are bound to the application of Mass for the people.[54] To the question, whether a *vicarius oeconomus,* who is taking charge of several parishes during the vacancy, is obliged to say only one Mass on the prescribed days for the several populations committed to his care, the Commission for the Interpretation of the Code answered in the affirmative, according to C. 473, 1, compared with C. 466, §2.[55]

ARTICLE II. PASTORS IN THE UNITED STATES

Canon 466 made it quite definite that pastors were bound by the law of the Code to the application of Mass for the people. However, it did leave the way open for some doubt as to the inclusion of those in the United States who were called pastors. There had been those who had denied the obligation for rulers of parishes particularly while this country was still under the jurisdiction of the Congregation for the Propagation of the Faith.[56] The discussion continued from the promulgation of the Code till 1922 as is evident from the number of questions on this point submitted to the two leading ecclesiastical publications of the United States.[57]

[52] S. C. C., *Principis Alberten. et Saskatoonen.*, 5 martii, 1932, ad II—*AAS*, XXV, 436; Bouscaren, *Canon Law Digest,* I, pp. 151-154.

[53] C. 473, §1.

[54] Augustine, *A Commentary on the New Code of Canon Law* (8 vols., St. Louis: Herder & Co., 1925-1938), II, 566, footnote 11. (Hereafter this work will be cited as *Commentary.*) Cocchi, *Commentarium,* III, n. 361; De Meester, *Compendium,* II, n. 869.

[55] Pontifical Commission for the Authentic Interpretation of the Canons of the Code (hereafter cited as *CIC*), 14 iulii, 1922, VI—*AAS,* XIV, 528.

[56] Cf. *Supra,* pp. 37-41.

[57] *Homiletic and Pastoral Review,* XIX (1919), 722; XX (1920), 124; 155; *Ecclesiastical Review,* LXVIII (1918), 563; LIX (1918), 304; LX (1919), 182; LXIII (1920), 343.

Among the reasons for holding that the obligation of pastors, as stated in canon 339, §1 did not apply in the United States were:

1. Pastors in the United States were not pastors in the canonical sense, since they were revocable *ad nutum*.

2. According to the II Plenary Council of Baltimore, article 124, they were merely quasi-pastors or mere representatives of the bishop and therefore at most they were obliged to say Mass for the people only on the days mentioned in canon 306.[58]

The question, therefore, hinged on the status of pastors and parishes in the United States. Parishes here seemed to some writers to lack the necessary formalities in establishment which were essential to give them the status as canonical parishes. Canon 216 stated that the territory of each diocese was to be divided into distinct territorial parts; each part was to be assigned its own church, its definite group of parishioners and its distinct rector. The canon stated further that the parts into which dioceses are divided in that manner are parishes.

But the Dioceses of the United States had been under the Sacred Congregation of the Propagation of the Faith until 1908, and their parishes were quasi-parishes. Did the promulgation of the Code *ipso facto* place "parishes" in this country into the class of canonical parishes? Canon 216 used the phrase *dividatur*, that is, it demanded that each diocese be divided into certain sections and that each section be made a parish. But the canon did not indicate that a change was effected in the canonical status of existing divisions. It did not appear likely that the Holy See would confer full parochial rights upon thousands of quasi-parishes or missions when the Code so carefully laid down the conditions required for the erection of any benefice and parish and implicitly demanded a close study of each case in particular.[59]

The prevailing opinion, however, maintained that pastors in the United States held true canonical parishes and that they were bound to the application of Mass for the people as set forth in

---

[58] *ER*, LX (1919), 182; *HPR*, XX (1920), 124.

[59] Ayrinhac, *Constitution of the Church*, p. 23.

canon 466, §1.[60] This opinion is well summed up in the *Ecclesiastical Review* in response to the question "Are our pastors obliged to say the *Missa pro populo,* according to canon 339, on all Sundays and feast days of obligation, including also those abrogated?" The response given was as follows:

> Until an authoritative decision is rendered, the conviction, unanimous so far as we can learn, among canonists who have written on the subject, is that an obligation exists. The conviction rests on an inference from canon 216, which declares that dioceses are to be divided into parishes, and Vicariates and Prefectures Apostolic into quasi parishes. The inference is that rectors of the division commonly called parishes are now, not *quasi-parochi* but *parochi.* If it should be declared that this was not the intention of the legislator, the inference, of course, is not a valid foundation for the conviction that the obligation in justice exists at the present time.[61]

This view was confirmed by a declaration of the Sacred Consistorial Congregation to the effect that in dioceses which, before the constitution *Sapienti consilio,* were under the jurisdiction of the Sacred Congregation of the Propagation of the Faith, but which thereafter were brought under the general law, these practical rules were to govern:

1. It is certain from canon 216, that such parts of these dioceses which have assigned to them a particular rector for the care of souls, are hereafter to be considered and called parishes, reserving the name quasi-parish or mission for those parts into which vicariates and prefectures apostolic are divided for the care of souls.

---

[60] "Quaer. 3—An sacerdotes qui apud nos curam habent animarum quoque nomine vocentur, praedicto onere teneantur? Resp. Tenentur quia sunt parochi vel quasi-parochi, cf. Conc. Plen. Balt. II, n. 367, canons 216, 415."—Sabetti-Barrett, *Compendium Theologiae Moralis* (ed. 27, New York, 1919), p. 653;

"There are no quasi-pastors in dioceses which are under the common law, only in dioceses and districts subject to the Congregation of Propaganda there are quasi-pastors, who need only to apply Mass for the people on the few feasts mentioned in can. 306."—Woywod, *HPR,* XX (1919–1920), 155.

[61] *ER,* LX (1919), 182–183.

2. To erect a parish a decree of the Ordinary is required defining the boundaries of its territory, assigning a parochial residence and fixing the endowment for public worship and the support of the priest.

3. When the erection of the parish has been completed as prescribed, the rector whether he be a pastor or an administrator, is bound to apply the Mass for the people.[62]

In spite of this declaration there still remained some uncertainty as to the status of parishes in this country.[63] The question was definitely settled in 1922 by a letter of the Apostolic Delegate to the bishops of the United States, concerning a private but official response of the Pontifical Commission for the Authentic Interpretation of the Canons of the Code.[64]

The Apostolic Delegate had submitted two questions:

For the erection of a parish which has not the character of a benefice:

1. is it necessary that the Ordinary should issue a decree declaring explicitly that he erects a certain district into a parish, or

2. is it sufficient that, having divided a certain territory into several districts, the respective limits of which are definitely indicated, he assigns to each district a rector to take charge of the people and the church thereto pertaining, according to canon 216, 1° and 3°?

Cardinal Gasparri, as president of the Commission, replied:

---

[62] S. C. Consist., Declaratio, 1 aug. 1919—*AAS,* XI, 346; Bouscaren, *Canon Law Digest,* I, 147.

[63] "Among these varied and unsettled conditions it is not always easy to apply the general law which constitutes a definite parish with the obligations of the *Missa pro populo.*"—*ER,* LXIII (1920), 346; cfr. also, Ayrinhac, *Constitution of the Church,* p. 24; Woywod, *A Practical Commentary on the Code,* I, n. 169.

[64] "Notwithstanding the fact that several years have elapsed since the promulgation of the new Code of Canon Law, there still seems to be some uncertainty in the United States as to the nature of the parishes in this country, and as to the consequent obligation of the pastors who are in charge of them. Both these questions have been debated in published articles from time to time. In order definitively to end this uncertainty, I deem it my duty to communicate to you an official answer which I received from the Pontifical Commission for the Authentic Interpretation of the Canons of the Code."—Bouscaren, *Canon Law Digest,* I, 150.

"Negative ad primam partem," i.e., that a special decree of the Ordinary is not necessary for the erection of a parish; and "affirmative ad secundam partem," i.e., that it is sufficient, *quoad hoc,* for the erection of a parish, that the Ordinary define the territorial limits and assign a rector to care for the people and the church within these limits. He added that a special decree of the Ordinary was not necessary to constitute as canonical parishes those which, previous to the promulgation of the new Code, had been established in the same manner as described in the second part of the question. Such parishes became canonical parishes *ipso facto* on the promulgation of the new Code.

The obvious conclusions derived from this statement of the Commission were stated by the letter of the Apostolic Delegate:

> It is evident from this official answer that all the parishes of the United States having the three necessary qualifications, viz., (1) a resident pastor; (2) endowment, [resources or revenue according to the provisions of canons 1410, 1415, §3] and (3) boundaries, are not only parishes in the strict canonical sense, but are also ecclesiastical benefices. Hence, pastors in the United States are real canonical pastors (parochi) having all the duties and obligations pertaining to such an office and (according to canons 466 and 339) are specifically bound to apply the Mass for the people on Sundays and on feast days of obligation (including those that have been suppressed), this obligation binding them in conscience unless dispensation or commutation be received from the Holy See.

This response did not speak of the status of national parishes in the United States. According to Woywod, since the Code recognizes the national parishes established before the Code was promulgated and forbids the local Ordinary to change them without consulting the Holy See, they may be considered canonical.[65] Ayrinhac says the conclusions from this answer do not apply to national parishes which have no strict boundaries.[66] If by this

[65] *Commentary,* I, n. 169.

[66] "It is evident from this official response that all the parishes in the United States having the three necessary qualifications are not only parishes in the strict canonical sense but also ecclesiastical benefices, and their

statement Ayrinhac means that the letter of the Apostolic Delegate cannot be applied to those national parishes which have no strict boundaries his statement is correct because these parishes would lack one of the three necessary qualifications. However, if his statement means that this does not apply to national parishes in general, since they have no strict boundaries, the statement is in error. National parishes, while their jurisdiction may cover the territory of several territorial parishes, are usually limited to a people speaking a certain language or of a certain nationality within a very definite geographical division. Pastors of national parishes with given geographical limits are certainly bound by the obligation of canon 466.[67]

ARTICLE III. THE OBLIGATION FOR ORIENTALS

The very opening canon of the Code states that the discipline of the Code does not bind the Oriental Church except in those things which derive from the divine law, or which, from the very nature of the subject matter affect the Oriental Church. The obligation of Mass for the people stems from divine precept and therefore in its substance it affects the Oriental Church. Therefore in the Oriental Church pastors of souls are bound to apply Mass for the people, but they are not strictly bound to observe the days determined by purely ecclesiastical law.[68] Not only under the prescriptions of canon 1 is this obligation evident but also under two pre-Code decrees. In response to a *dubium* of 1863, the Sacred Congregation of the Propagation of the Faith decided:

1. That the obligation of applying Mass for the people which

---

pastors have all the obligations of canonical pastors. This does not apply to national parishes which have no strict boundaries."—Ayrinhac, *Constitution of the Church*, p. 25.

[67] "Contention that rectors of Churches which have been organized for the benefit of a foreign speaking congregation are not pastors and are not obliged to say the Missa pro populo does not hold."—*ER*, LIX (1918), 304.

[68] Prümmer, *Theologia Moralis*, III, n. 254; Marc-Gestermann, I, *Institutiones Morales*, n. 1606, I; Blat, *Commentarium Textus Codicis Iuris Canonici* (5 vols. in 7, Romae: Collegio "Anglico," 1921–1938), II, 363. (Hereafter this work will be cited as *Commentarium*.) Cicognani, *Canon Law* (2 ed. English version, Philadelphia, 1935), pp. 454, 455.

according to the law of the Western Church is imposed on bishops and priests is incumbent equally on the same persons of the Oriental Church;

2. That in the determination of the days on which Mass is to be applied, there should be observed the laws and reasonable customs which may flourish in dioceses of the Oriental Rite;

3. That in the absence of such laws and customs the determination of the days need not be made according to the norm and exactly according to the laws of the Western Church;

4. That with regard to a reduction in the number of these days and even to total dispensation, the rule in the Western Church need not be followed, but the mind of the Congregation is that the rule be made known to bishops of the Oriental Church so that they may judge whether similar discipline would be adaptable in their dioceses and may propose to the Holy See whatever adjustments they think necessary in each case.[69] This response made the doctrine and discipline rather clear. However, when the *In suprema* of Leo XIII appeared, the Sacred Congregation decided to remove any possible doubts and for that purpose addressed an encyclical letter to the Apostolic Delegate for the Oriental Church. This letter not only contained a clear exposition of the duties of priests and bishops of the Oriental Church in regard to the Mass for the people, but also supported it with an excellent résumé of the nature of the obligation itself. First of all it stated that the letter was the result of an examination by the Cardinals of the Sacred Congregation of the subject, "the obligation of applying the Mass for the people among the Orientals." The letter contained the following rules:

1. According to the decretal of Innocent III, *Licet Graecos,* in the IV Lateran Council, and according to an exposition of its meaning given in 1631 by a group of theologians, with Cardinal Pamphili presiding, most doctors, not excluding Lambertini himself, believe that Apostolic constitutions do not bind the Orientals except in three cases:

(a) in points of Catholic faith and doctrine.

(b) where the matter is, from its nature, not only an ec-

---

[69] S. C. de Prop. Fidei, 23 martii 1863—*Collectanea, S. C. P. F.*, n. 1238.

clesiastical law, but also a declaration of the divine natural law.

(c) when in disciplinary matters the Orientals are explicitly named.

2. It is certain that, from time immemorial, the Orientals themselves have held that, as a theoretical and practical opinion, they are not bound by the disciplinary constitutions of the Holy See except in the aforesaid manner.

3. It is clear that all bishops, even those of the Oriental Church, are included in the constitution *In suprema* insofar as it declares the divine law of the obligation of the Mass for the people, since by reason of their pastoral office bishops of any rite are so held *de jure divino*.

4. This is not a point of changeable discipline which can be modified or abolished in the different rites by contrary custom, insofar as it treats of the obligation of bishops *in se* of offering Mass for the people.

5. The number of Masses to be applied is determined by the ecclesiastical law in application of the divine law, and in this matter diversity of discipline or dispensation is not excluded according to varying circumstances.

Therefore, bishops and priests of the Oriental Church are bound by the leg'slation of the Code in this matter only insofar as it contains the divine law, but the ecclesiastical determination of the precept is left to the individual rite.

ARTICLE IV. THOSE HAVING THE CARE OF SOULS UNDER MULTIPLE TITLE

C. 339, 5.—Licet Episcopus duas vel plures dioeceses aeque principaliter unitas regat aut, praeter propriam dioecesim, aliam vel alias in administrationem habeat, obligationi tamen satisfacit per celebrationem et applicationem unius Missae pro universo populo sibi commisso.

C. 466, 2.—Parochus qui plures forte paroecias aeque principaliter unitas regat aut, praeter propriam paroeciam, aliam vel alias in administrationem habeat, unam tantum debet Missam pro populis sibi commissis diebus praescriptis applicare.

While the obligation of applying the Mass for the people binds under divine law all who have the care of souls, the determination of this obligation and its application to specific classes of pastors is contained in the ecclesiastical law. Ecclesiastical law may therefore legislate for those cases in which an individual has the care of souls under more than one title as it does in Canons 339 and 466:

(a) A bishop who rules two or more dioceses as independent entities (i.e., aequi-principally united), or besides his own dioceses administers another or several others, need say only one Mass on the specified days for his flock.

(b) A pastor who rules two or more parishes as independent entities (i.e., aequi-principally united), or besides his own parish administers another or several others, need say only one Mass on the specified days for his whole flock.

(c) The Pontifical Commission for the Authentic Interpretation of the Code applied this principle also to an administrator (*vicarius oeconomus*) who is taking charge of several parishes during the vacancy. He is obliged to say only one Mass on the prescribed days for the several peoples committed to his care.[70]

(d) A bishop who is also the pastor of the Cathedral parish has the concomitant obligation of offering the Mass for the people of that parish. He does not satisfy the duty to which he is bound as pastor by the application of Mass for his diocesans.[71] The existence of the obligation to offer one Mass for the people of the parish and another for the people of the diocese is clearly deducible from a decision of the Sacred Congregation of the Propagation of the Faith.[72] The bishop of Dromore held also the parish of Newry. The Congregation ruled that if the bishop had not appointed a vicar to administer the parish of Newry, he would have to make provision for one, and through him discharge the obligation of the Mass for the people of the parish.[73]

Among the days on which a pastor must apply the Mass for

---

[70] CIC, 14 iul. 1922, ad VI—*AAS*, XIV, 528.

[71] S. C. de Prop. Fide, 23 martii 1863—*Collectanea S. Congregationis de Propaganda Fide* (Romae ex Typographia Polyglotta Vaticana, 1907), n. 1239. (Hereafter this work will be cited as *Collectanea S. C. P. F.*)

[72] *Op. cit., loc. cit.*

[73] *ER*, LXX (1924), p. 633; cf. also p. 313.

the people is the feast of the patron saint of the place. What is the duty of a pastor who has charge of several parishes in different places, each of which has a different patron whose feasts occur on different days? The Sacred Congregation of the Council decided that the pastor is then obliged to offer the Mass for the people on each of the feasts.[74]

What of the case of bishops who rule one diocese and administer another or others? If these dioceses have individual patrons, are the bishops bound to apply the Mass for the people on the feasts of each of these patrons? There is no explicit law on this matter but in view of the response regarding pastors, it is legitimately deduced that bishops in such circumstances are bound to apply the Mass for the people on the feast of each patron.

It may be noted that section 5 of canon 339 and section 2 of canon 466 are practically identical. Yet the necessity for the explicit provision in both cases is evident because the Code in its legislation on bishops who rule more than one diocese is merely repeating the old law while its legislation on pastors who rule more than one parish is a departure from previous discipline. Canon 339, §5 is taken from the Apostolic letter of Leo XIII, *In suprema.*[75]

---

[74] S. C. C., *Blesen.*, 12 nov. 1927—*AAS*, XX, 84.

[75] "Et ne cui dubitationi aditus pateat, declaramus eosdem episcopos et abbates huic officio satis esse facturos per celebrationem et applicationem unius Missae pro universo populo sibi commisso, etiamsi duas vel plures dioecesis et abbatias aeque principaliter unitas regant."—Leo XIII, litt. apost. "In suprema"—*Fontes*, 585.

CHAPTER VI

The Days on Which the Obligation Binds

ARTICLE I. A RESTRICTED LIST OF DAYS FOR VICARS AND PREFECTS APOSTOLIC, AND QUASI-PASTORS

The subjects of the obligation can be divided into two groups according to the days on which they are bound to apply the Mass.

Vicars and Prefects Apostolic, and quasi-pastors are bound to apply Mass for the people committed to them on eleven days in the year, namely the feasts of the Nativity of Our Lord, the Epiphany, Easter, the Ascension, Pentecost, Corpus Christi, the Immaculate Conception, the Assumption, St. Joseph, SS. Peter and Paul, and All Saints.[1] Cappello in one place says that quasi-pastors are bound only on the ten days which are assigned for Vicars and Prefects Apostolic, but this is evidently a misprint for in another place he says that Vicars and Prefects Apostolic are bound to apply Mass for the people on eleven more solemn feasts.[2]

ARTICLE II. DAYS ON WHICH RESIDENTIAL BISHOPS, VICARS CAPITULAR, AND PASTORS ARE BOUND

A. *Sundays and Feasts of Precept.* All other subjects of the obligation besides those mentioned above in article one are bound to apply Mass for the people on every Sunday and feast of precept, even though it be suppressed.[3] There are ten feasts of precept for the universal Church, namely the feasts of the Na-

[1] Cc. 306, 466, §1.

[2] Quasi parochi tenentur dumtaxat illis *decem* diebus qui pro vicariis et praefectis apostolicis can. 306 assignati sunt."—Cappello, *Summa Iuris Canonici* (ed. altera, Romae: Apud Aedes Universitatis Gregorianae, 1932–1936), II, n. 528. (Hereafter this work will be cited as *Summa.*)

"Vicarii et praefecti tenentur Sacrum applicare pro populo undecim solemnioribus festis."—Cappello, *Summa,* I, n. 351.

[3] C. 339, §1.

tivity of Our Lord, the Epiphany, the Ascension, Corpus Christi, the Immaculate Conception, the Assumption, St. Joseph, SS. Peter and Paul, and All Saints.[4] It is to be noted that these are the feasts of precept for the Universal Church. On these days there is an obligation of applying the Mass for the people, even if in a particular place one or more of the days is not observed as of obligation. Thus in the United States only the Sundays and six of the feasts are of obligation under a decree of the Sacred Congregation of the Propagation of the Faith, namely the feasts of the Immaculate Conception, the Nativity of our Lord, the Circumcision, the Ascension, the Assumption, and All Saints.[5] Yet the obligation of applying the Mass for the people remains even on those days which are not of precept in this country.[6]

Local Ordinaries have the power of establishing, for their own dioceses or places, feast days which are to be established only temporarily, not forever or habitually.[7] Such days would not be included among those to which is attached the obligation of Mass for the people, since they are not strictly the feasts of precept of canon 339.[8] If however, from a concession of the Holy See, a particular feast of precept is celebrated in a diocese, there is imposed an obligation on those with the care of souls in that place of applying Mass for the people on that day.[9] Blat disagrees with this conclusion. He says that the phrase "diebus festis de precepto, etiam suppressis" must be understood only of the days of precept for the Universal Church. His reason is that Leo

[4] C. 1247. §1.

[5] Cf. *Acta et Decreta Conc. Balt. III* (1886, Baltimorae), cvi.

[6] "If in any part of the Church any of the ten feasts which, according to canon 1247 are of obligation throughout the whole Church, are in fact not observed as days of obligation, nevertheless bishops and priests will be under the obligation of saying Mass on those days for their people."—Slater, "The Mass Pro Populo"—*ER*, LXI (1920), 634-640; cf. also Koudelka, *Pastors, Their Rights and Duties*, p. 46; Woywod, *HPR*, XX (1919), 777-778.

[7] C. 1244, §2.

[8] Cappello, *De Sacramentis*, I, n. 646.

[9] Wernz-Vidal, *Ius Canonicum*, II, n. 604; Aertnys-Damen, *Theologia Moralis*, I, n. 1146; Cocchi, *Commentarium*, III, n. 261, B, b; Cappello, *Summa*, I, n. 380; *De Sacramentis*, I, n. 644; Ferreres, *Institutiones Canonicae* (ed. altera, 2 vols., Barcinone, 1920), I, n. 652.

XIII and Pius IX in designating in their Apostolic Letters the days for the observance of this obligation recalled the constitution *Universa* of Urban VIII which designated both Sundays and days of universal precept, and at the same time exhorted bishops that they abstain from proclaiming particular feasts.[10] Blat's opinion is not tenable. Besides the weight of authorities ranged against him, there is a response of the Sacred Congregation of the Council. It is a particular response, obliging only the bishops and pastors of the place to which it was given, but it furnishes confirmation of the view that the phrase "diebus festis de praecepto, etiam suppressis," applies also to feasts of obligation instituted by Apostolic authority for a particular place. To a question of the Cardinal Archbishop of Toledo whether the obligation of applying Mass for the people on suppressed feasts which were formerly of obligation in virtue of particular law exists in this case, the reply was, "In the affirmative." [11] As a matter of fact, Blat's reference to the two Papal constitutions exhorting Bishops to abstain from proclaiming particular feasts does not touch the particular question here, for the feasts considered are those established for a particular place by the Holy See.

B. *Suppressed Feasts.* After the promulgation of the Code there was some question as to just what suppressed feasts were referred to in Canon 339. Pope Urban VIII, by his Bull *Universa* had begun the work of reduction and suppression of the days on which the faithful were bound to hear Mass and rest from servile work.[12] Other Popes, among them Pius VI,[13] and Pius VIII,[14] had suppressed other feasts. Pius IX had stated that Mass must be applied on those days which had formerly been holy days, according to the Constitution of Urban VIII, but which later were suppressed by various indults of the Holy See.[15]

---

[10] Blat, *Commentarium,* II, n. 363.

[11] S. C. C., *Toletana et aliarum,* 19 iulii, 1930—*AAS,* XXII, 521.

[12] Urbanus VIII, const. *Universa,* 13 sept. 1642—*Bullarium Romanum* XV, 206–208.

[13] Pallottini, v. "*Parochus,*" VI, n. 83.

[14] *Bullarii Romani continuatio,* XII, 1712.

[15] Pius IX, litt. encycl. *Amantissimi Redemptoris,* 3 maii 1858—*Fontes,* n. 525.

In 1911 Pius X also suppressed certain feasts.[16] The Sacred Congregation of the Council decided that the obligation of applying for the people remained even on those feasts suppressed *quoad forum* by Pius X in his *Supremi disciplinae,* namely the feasts of Corpus Christi, the Purification, Annunication and Nativity of Our Lady, St. Joseph, St. John the Evangelist, and the Patron of the place or of the diocese.[17] This plurality of suppressions furnished the reason for the question: "What are the suppressed feasts which are referred to in canons 339, §1 and 466, §1, on which bishops and pastors must apply Mass for the people committed to their care?" The answer of the Pontifical Commission for the Authentic Interpretation of the Canons of the Code was that the Code of Canon Law made no change in this matter from the discipline that had hitherto been in effect.[18] Still there remained some doubt. Was that discipline to be considered as exemplified in the *Motu proprio* of Pius X, or in the feasts of precept set forth in the time-honored list of Urban VIII and since suppressed? Or did it refer to general feasts to be suppressed in the future? A new question was sent, this time to the Sacred Congregation of the Council, asking for a list of the suppressed feasts to which Canon 339 referred. This list was given on December 28, 1918.[19]

C. *List of Days.* According to this authentic list, in the universal Church there is an obligation of applying Mass for the people on 52 Sundays of the year, 10 feasts of precept, 26 suppressed feasts. The list of these days follows:

1–52. All Sundays of the year—fifty-two.
53. Circumcision ....Jan. 1
54. Epiphany ....Jan. 6
55. Purification of the Blessed Virgin..............Feb. 2
56. St. Matthias ....Feb. 24
57. St. Joseph ....March 19
58. Annunciation of the Blessed Virgin ....March 25
59. The Monday after Easter.

[16] Pius X, motu propr. *Supremi disciplinae,* 2 iul. 1911—*AAS,* III, 391.
[17] S. C. C. *Romana et aliarum,* 8 aug., 1911—*AAS,* III, 391.
[18] CIC, 17 feb. 1918—*AAS,* X, 170.
[19] S. C. C., 28 dec., 1918—*AAS,* XII, 42.

60. The Tuesday after Easter.
61. SS. Philip and James .... May 1
62. Finding of the Cross .... May 3
63. Ascension.
64. Monday after Pentecost.
65. Tuesday after Pentecost.
66. Corpus Christi.
67. Nativity of St. John the Baptist.............. June 24
68. SS. Peter and Paul .... June 29
69. St. James .... July 25
70. St. Anne .... July 26
71. St. Lawrence .... Aug. 10
72. Assumption of the Blessed Virgin............ Aug. 15
73. St. Bartholemew .... Aug. 24
74. Nativity of the Blessed Virgin .... Sept. 8
75. St. Matthew .... Sept. 21
76. Dedication of St. Michael, the Archangel...... Sept. 29
77. SS. Simon and Jude .... Oct. 28
78. All Saints .... Nov. 1
79. St. Andrew .... Nov. 30
80. Immaculate Conception of the Blessed Virgin... Dec. 8
81. St. Thomas .... Dec. 21
82. Nativity of Our Lord .... Dec. 25
83. St. Stephen .... Dec. 26
84. St. John .... Dec. 27
85. Holy Innocents .... Dec. 28
86. St. Sylvester .... Dec. 31
87. Patron of the Country.
88. Patron of the Place.

In the United States the number is reduced by one because the feast of the Immaculate Conception, which under canon 1247 is a holy day of obligation, is also the Patronal feast of the Country.[20] It is interesting to note that Augustine in his 1936 edition makes no mention of the list of suppressed feasts given by the Sacred Congregation of the Council. He states that the days on which a bishop is obliged to say Mass for the people are Sundays, holy days of obligation, celebrated *in foro et in choro,* and such suppressed feasts as are now celebrated only *in choro.* In both his 1919 and 1936 editions he lists six feasts *in foro et in choro,*

[20] Decretum IV, ex Aed. S. Congregationis de Propaganda Fide, die 24 januarii, 1868—*Concilium Plenarium Baltimorense II, Acta et Decreta,* p. lxxiv.

and twenty-five suppressed feasts, omitting from his list the feasts of St. Anne, St. Lawrence, St. Bartholomew, the patron of the place and the patron of the country.[21] It is to be noted that, in addition to this list of eighty-eight days, the Mass for the people is also to be offered on those days which were formerly of obligation for a particular place, by particular law but under an Apostolic rescript and are now suppressed.[22]

D. *Feasts of Patrons of Places.* What is meant by the feast of the patron of the place? The Code does not explain, nor does the response of the Sacred Congregation of the Council do more than give the phrase "dies S. Patroni loci." [23] Yet the Pontifical Commission made it clear that the Code introduced no change in the pre-existing law in this regard.[24] A writer in the *Ecclesiastical Review* states that since no change was made in the days on which the obligation binds light will be thrown on this question by referring to the Constitution of Urban VIII, *Universa,* of September 13, 1642. Therefore this writer denies that the feast of the patron of the diocese is included in the "dies S. Patroni loci." His argument is that the Constitution clearly distinguishes between the patronal feast of a city, town or village, and feasts binding in a diocese, and clearly abolishes the latter, i.e., only the patronal feast of a city, town or village remained a holy day of obligation. Therefore, it was only on the patronal feast of a city, town or village that there was an obligation of applying the Mass for the people, but not on the patronal feast of a diocese. That should be the rule even after the promulgation of the Code. For the obligation of applying the Mass for the people binds only on those days which, though now suppressed, were of obligation at any time since the constitution of Urban VIII.[25] Pauwels agrees at least with the conclusion that the "patron saint of a place" cannot include the patron of the diocese.[26] But while the pre-

---

[21] Augustine, *A Commentary on the New Code of Canon Law,* vol. II (3 ed., 1919), 363; vol. II (6 revised edition, 1936), 363.

[22] S. C. C., Resolutio, *Toletana et aliarum,* 19 iulii, 1930—*AAS,* XXII, 521.

[23] S. C. C., 28 dec. 1918—*AAS,* XII, 42.

[24] CIC, 17 feb., 1918—*AAS,* X, 170.

[25] *The Ecclesiastical Review,* XC (1934), 428.

[26] ". . . et in die S. Patroni Regni, nec non in festo S. Patroni loci (h. e.

Code discipline in general measured the suppressed feasts by the constitution of Urban VIII, there was a response issued later than this constitution regarding patronal feasts, and it is rather this that should be considered as constituting the prevailing discipline from which the Code made no change.

The Sacred Congregation of Rites in 1857 [27] decided that the patron of a place, strictly speaking, is that saint whom a certain state, *diocese,* province, or realm, chooses as its special patron with God, preserving in this choice the rules laid down in the decree of Urban VIII on March 23, 1630.[28] This decree provided that the patron must be a canonized saint, not merely a beatified person; must be chosen by the people of the place through the medium of the general council of the state or place, not by the officials only; and must be approved by the local bishop and clergy.

The patron of the place may also, however, be declared by Apostolic letter containing a dispensation from the formalities prescribed by the above decrees.[29] Examples of this Apostolic intervention are the letters of Pius XI.[30]

Therefore in view of the decree of the Sacred Congregation of Rites, it is evident that the patron of a place is:

1. a saint,
2. whom a certain state, diocese, province or realm has chosen as its special patron;
3. by action of the people,
4. with the approval of the local bishop and clergy.

This does not necessarily mean the titular saint of the parish or cathedral church unless he has been chosen according to the conditions laid down. It is doubtful whether even in the early

---

civitatis, vel oppidi non autem diocesis) iuxta praescriptum c. 339, §1, can. 466, §1 pastores pro grege celebrare tenentur." Cf. *AAS,* 2 feb. 1920, XII (1920), 42.

[27] S. R. C., *in Briocen,* 9 maii, 1857—*Decreta Authentica,* n. 3048; cfr. also *AAS,* XX (1928), 84, n. 2.

[28] S. R. C. 23 martii, 1630—*Decreta Authentica,* n. 526.

[29] Bouscaren, *Canon Law Digest,* I, 256.

[30] Pius XI, litt., 24 aug., 1930—*AAS,* XXIII, 154. Litt., 8 sept. 1930—*AAS,* XXIII, 156.

French or Spanish settlements of this country a choice of a patron saint was made for any city, town or village in that manner. Hence it is to be doubted whether there is any political unit in the United States that has a duly chosen patron saint on whose feast the obligation of applying Mass for the people would bind a pastor. But if anywhere a patron of a diocese had been chosen according to the proper norms, the obligation would bind on the feast day of that patron.[31] Woywod indeed feels that there may be some towns in this country where a patron was legitimately chosen.[32]

ARTICLE III. APPLICATION WHEN THERE IS MULTIPLICATION OR TRANSFER OF OBLIGATION

> Canon 339, 2.—In festo Nativitatis Domini, et si quod festum de praecepto in diem dominicam incidat, satis est ut Missam unam pro populo applicent.
>
> 3.—Si festum ita transfertur ut in die *ad quem* non solum fiat officium cum Missa festi translati sed serventur quoque obligationes audiendi Missam et abstinendi a servilibus Missa pro populo applicanda est in die *ad quem;* secus in die *a quo.*

In addition to indicating the days on which Mass for the people is to be applied, the canons also give the rule to be followed when two of these days coincided or when a feast is transferred:

1. If a feast of precept falls on a Sunday, it is sufficient that one Mass be applied,
2. On the feast of the Nativity it is sufficient that one Mass be applied,
3. If a feast is so transferred that on the day *to which* it is transferred, not only the Mass and the Office, but also the obligation of hearing Mass and the duty to abstain from servile work are transferred, Mass for the people is to be applied on the day *to which* the feast is transferred;

---

[31] *ER*, XC (1934), 428.

[32] Patrons of towns and cities are practically unknown here in the United States, except in some places in the districts first settled by the Spanish and French where a patron of a town had been legitimately chosen."—Woywod, *Commentary,* I, 123.

4. If a feast is so transferred that either the Office or the obligation of hearing Mass, or the duty to abstain from servile work is not transferred, the Mass for the people is to be applied on the day *from which* the Mass of the feast is transferred.

Cappello mentions two possible situations in which the feast would be only transferred partly.

(a) When feasts of precept are transferred to the following Sunday while the Office and the Mass are said on the appointed day, as is not infrequent in France.

(b) When the Office and the Mass are transferred, but the feast is celebrated on the assigned day.[33]

In the United States no feast day or holy day of obligation is ever transferred.[34] But what of the transfer of suppressed feasts on which there is an obligation of offering Mass for the people? Suppose the office and Mass of such a feast is transferred? There can be no transfer of the obligations of hearing Mass and abstaining from servile work since these obligations no longer exist on such feasts. Is the Mass for the people to be applied on the day *to which* the feast is transferred, or on the day *from which* it is transferred? From the words of the canon it is evident that the Mass for the people is to be offered on the day *from which* the transfer is made. The canon uses the phrase, " Si . . . serventur quoque obligationes audiendi Missam et abstinendi a servilibus," and certainly in the case mentioned these two obligations are not "preserved." Hence in this country what may happen is that the Divine Office and the Mass of feasts like that of St. Joseph or the Annunciation may have to be transferred, but the application of the Mass for the people remains attached to the day on which the feast originally fell.

However there can be a real difficulty in those cases where the feast of the Annunciation or the feast of the patron of the place falls on Holy Thursday, Good Friday, or Holy Saturday. In such cases the Mass and the Office of the feast are transferred to the Monday after Low Sunday. When is the Mass for the people to be applied? When it is a case of Holy Thursday or Holy

---

[33] Cappello, *De Sacramentis,* I, n. 647.

[34] Woywod, *HPR,* XL (1940), 1239; *Commentary,* I, 121.

Saturday, the case should be solved as just indicated. For only the Office and Mass of the feast are transferred, and there is no transfer of the obligations of hearing Mass and abstaining from servile work. Mass for the people would be offered on the twenty-fifth of March (when the feast involved is the Annunciation) whether that day marked Holy Thursday or Holy Saturday. The same principle should apply also when the feast occurs on Good Friday, but the difficulty in that case arises from the fact that Mass is not said on that day. What then of the obligation of applying Mass for the people when the twenty-fifth of March is also Good Friday?

Vermeersch lists three opinions:

(a) The obligation ceases that year;

(b) Mass for the people is offered on the day *to which* the Mass and office of the feast of the Annunciation is transferred;

(c) Mass is to be offered for the people on the first free day.[35] Vermeersch himself holds the second opinion, namely that the Mass for the people is to be said on the day *to which* the Mass and Office of the feast of the Annunciation is transferred, the Monday after Low Sunday. He was writing about the approaching year of 1932 and he gave the date of that Monday as April fourth. His reasons follow:

1. The determination of the day on which Mass for the people is to be offered rests between the day *from which* and the day *to which* the Annunciation has been transferred. It cannot be the day *from which* since that is an *aliturgical* day, a day on which Mass is not offered. In such a case there is only one day which is properly the feast of the Annunciation, that is the day *to which* it is transferred, and therefore on that day Mass for the people must be applied.

2. A pre-Code decree, issued when the feast of the Annunciation was a holy day of obligation, provided that Mass for the people was to be offered on the day *to which* the feast is transferred. At that time the *feriatio* of the feast, that is, the obligations attaching to it as a holy day of obligation, was also transferred. Since there is no *feriatio,* that is, no obligation of hearing Mass

[35] Vermeersch, "Applicatio Missae pro populo quando in die propria nequit applicari."—*Periodica,* XXI (1932), 162*.

and abstaining from servile work attached to the feast today, there should be no consideration given it, but the other part of the decree of 1690 alone should be respected, that is, the transfer of Mass for the people.[36] This view, he argues, is more certain from the fact that canon 6, 4° warns us that in doubt we are not to recede from the old law. Further, the Commission for the Interpretation of the Code expressly declared that in regard to the feasts on which Mass for the people was to be applied, the Code made no change in the previous discipline.

3. Vermeersch notes that Haegy holds this view as certain, while an author in the *Ephemerides Liturgicae* advised that in the *ordo* to be drawn up, according to the calendar of the universal Church for the year 1932, the sign for the Mass for the people be placed opposite the date of April 4 (i.e., the Monday after Low Sunday, to which the Office and Mass of the Annunciation were transferred that year).

This is also the view of Pagan who states that it is the more common opinion.[37]

The weight of authority, however, rests with the view that under such circumstances the obligation of applying Mass for the people on the feast of the Annunciation ceases that year. Chelodi,[38] Coronata,[39] Fanfani,[40] De Meester,[41] Davis,[42] Cappello,[43] and Toso [44] support this view. The reasons in defense of the opinion, as given by Cappello, are as in the following:

1. Two conditions are required in canon 339, §3 in order that the duty of applying Mass for the people should be transferred to the day *to which* the feast is transferred; namely, first, that the

---

[36] Cf. S. C. R., 11 feb., 1690—*Decret. Authent.*, §1822 (3202).

[37] Pagan, "Messa pro populo nelle feste soppresse"—*Perfice Munus,* V (1930), 663-664.

[38] *Ius de Personis,* n. 192.

[39] *Institutiones,* I, n. 397, f.

[40] *De Iure Parochorum,* n. 370, dubium V.

[41] *Compendium,* II, n. 847.

[42] *Moral Theology,* III, 107.

[43] Cappello, "De Missa Pro Populo quando festum Annuntiationis B. M. V. incidat in feriam V, VI, vel Sabbatum hebdomadae maioris"—*Periodica,* XXI (1932), 146.

[44] Toso, *Commentaria Minora,* can. 466.

Mass and Office be transferred; second, that, in addition, there be a transfer also of the obligation of hearing Mass and of abstaining from servile work. If, for any reason, this second condition is lacking, the obligation of applying the Mass for the people is not transferred but remains affixed to the day from which the Mass and Office are moved.

2. If the feast of the Annunciation falls on Good Friday the Office and the Mass are indeed transferred. But by what law and title will any one say that the obligation of the Mass for the people is also transferred? Where does the Code prescribe such a transfer?

3. It is no argument to say that unless such a transfer is admitted the people are deprived of the application of a Mass that year. They are also deprived of a Mass when a feast of precept falls on Sunday, and this deprivation is explicitly sanctioned in the Code.

The more correct opinion, and therefore the opinion to be endorsed, is that of Cappello, namely that when the twenty-fifth of March, the feast of the Annunciation, is also Good Friday, the obligation of applying Mass for the people on the feast of the Annunciation ceases for that year. Vermeersch's argument that the question rests between two days on which the Mass for the people is to be offered, and that since it cannot be the first, or the *dies a quo,* as Mass is not offered on that day, it must be the day *to which* the Office is transferred, is not sound. It assumes as pròved that which is to be proved. Further, the pre-Code response to which he refers dealt with a feast of precept, not, as is now the case, with a suppressed feast. Nor is the matter affected by the declaration of the Commission for the Interpretation of the Code that through the Code there was nothing changed in this matter from the former discipline. The "in hac re" of that response referred simply and solely to the matter about which the Commission had been asked, namely, "What are the suppressed feasts which are referred to in canons 339, §1 and 466, §1, on which bishops and pastors must apply the Mass for the people committed to their care?" [45]

---

[45] *CIC*, 17 feb., 1918—*AAS*, X, 170.

Further the authority of Haegy and the *Ephemerides Liturgicae* cannot be invoked without reservation in favor of Vermeersch's opinion. Haegy says that the obligation of the Mass for the people would be transferred with the Office in the exceptional case in which the transfer involves the Office and the Mass and also the *feriatio* (that is assistance at Mass and abstinence from servile work), for example when the feast of the Annunciation falls on Good Friday or Holy Saturday. But it is not an example of a day on which the *feriatio* is transferred together with the Mass and Office.[46] The author in the *Ephemerides Liturgicae* does advise the insertion of the + in the *Ordo* for the date of April 4, 1932, as a sign indicating the obligation of Mass for the people on that day. But he does so only after he has given an answer of " Non constare," to the question "on which day, March 25 or April 4, is there an obligation of applying Mass for the people?" He closes his response with a wish that this doubt may be settled authentically by the Holy See for the tranquillity of consciences.[47] Woywod also arrives at the opinion of Cappello, but merely as a norm for practice. " Each (Vermeersch and Cappello) has his own reasons and neither seems to be conclusive enough to establish either opinion as certain; wherefore *indubiis libertas*." [48] Vermeersch notes that this case of the occurrence of the feast of the Annunciation on Good Friday will not occur again until the year 2006. But the principle established is of some importance since it applies equally when a patronal feast occurs on Good Friday.

The importance of the accurate determination of the days on which the subjects of the obligation are bound to offer Mass for the people rests on the fact that the obligation is a real one. Therefore if a Mass is omitted even in good faith it must be later supplied or a condonation obtained. Hence one who omitted a particular day for the application would incur an obligation to restitution.

---

46 Haegy, *Manuel de Liturgie et Ceremonial*, I, 169.

47 "Optamus autem ut hujusmodi dubium authentice a Sancta Sede dirimatur ad conscientiarum tranquillitatem."—*Ephemerides Liturgicae* (1931), 417.

48 Woywod, *HPR*, XL, 1239.

CHAPTER VII

Excusing Causes

Canon 339, _§4._—Episcopus Missam pro populo diebus supra indicatis per se ipse applicare debet; si ab ejus celebratione legitime impediatur, statis diebus applicet per alium; si neque id praestare possit, quamprimum vel per se ipse vel per alium applicet alia die.

_§6._—Episcopus, qui obligatione de qua in superioribus paragraphis non satisfecerit, quam citius pro populo tot applicet Missas quot omisit.

Canon 466, _§1._—Applicandae Missae pro populo obligatione tenetur parochus ad normam can. 339, quasiparochus ad normam can. 306.

§3.—Ordinarius loci iusta de causa permittere potest ut parochus Missam pro populo alia die applicet ab ea qua iure adstringitur.

_§4._—Parochus Missam pro populo applicandam celebret in ecclesia paroeciali, nisi rerum adiuncta Missam alibi celebrandam exigant aut suadeant.

_§5._—Legitime absens parochus potest Missam pro populo applicare vel ipse per se in loco in quo degit, vel per sacerdotem qui eius vices gerat in paroecia.

ARTICLE I. THE CAUSES PERMITTED BY THE CANONS

A. *Excusing Causes in General.* The obligation of offering Mass for the people is such that there is no excusing cause which would extinguish this obligation, even for a single instance.[1] The Code makes this clear in canon 339, §6 where it rules that a bishop who has not satisfied the obligation is to apply as soon as possible as many Masses for the people as he has omitted. Therefore a Mass for the people, omitted even in good faith, must be supplied or a commutation obtained. In its legislation for

[1] "Nulla causa eximit a Missa applicanda: nec redituum exiguitas, nec paupertas, nec infirmitas nec consuetudo centenaria, nec alia ulla excusatio allegari potest. Neque cessat obligatio propter omissionem culpabilem vel inculpabilem."—Cappello, *Summa,* I, 467, 5°.

bishops the Code insists that every excuse, whether based on a small income or any other exception, is to be rejected. In this sense the obligation is a *real* one, that is, the obligation remains until it has been satisfied. He who neglects it is guilty of a sin of injustice. Vermeersch asks whether a bishop who is prevented from the personal celebration by illness or other legitimate impediment is bound to have the Mass said by another for a stipend. He answers that the decision depends on whether or not the bishop receives income from his *mensa* or from any other source as compensation for the burdens of his administration.[2] If by this statement Vermeersch means, as seems evident, that a bishop who is legitimately impeded from the personal celebration of the Mass, is excused from the real obligation because of lack of income from his office, he is wrong, as is quite clear from canon 339, §6. If, however, he means that in such circumstances the bishop is justified in putting off the application of the Mass for the people until such time as he himself is able to celebrate it, the statement may stand.

There are secondary characteristics of the obligation for which excusing causes are possible. The obligation is *personal*—so that the one bound to the application of the Mass for the people is bound to apply it himself. The Code makes clear the personal nature of the obligation in saying that the bishop ought to apply Mass for the people on the days indicated *per se ipse,* and that the pastor is bound to apply according to the norm of canon 339.[3] But this requirement is not so rigid that it cannot admit of excuse for sufficient cause. What is a sufficient cause? The phrase the canon uses with regard to the bishop—if he is legitimately impeded—leaves the problem of determining what constitutes a legitimate impediment. It is to be noted that the canon says, impeded from the celebration not from the *application.* This might seem to indicate that the only excusing causes adduced should be those which would prevent the subject of the obligation from *celebrating* Mass, not those which would prevent him merely from *applying* Mass for the people. Augustine, however, says explicitly that the phrase does not restrict the excuse to the case in which a bishop

[2] Vermeersch, *Theologia Moralis,* III, n. 83, 6o.

[3] c. 339, §4; c. 466, §1.

is unable to say Mass at all, but extends it to the case in which he is not able to apply Mass for this intention.[4] Coronata mentions this interpretation of Augustine and says that it seems probable.[5] Others who hold this view are Blat and Kaiser.[6] In addition, the Code states that one who, on the same day is bound by the obligation of both a conventual Mass and the Mass for the people, is to celebrate and apply the conventual Mass personally, and apply the Mass for the people through another or personally on the following day.[7] This is an example of a case in which a pastor is impeded from *applying* Mass for the people and not from *celebrating*. The Code here recognizes this as a legitimate impediment. From this fact it is evident that the Code in canon 466 includes a legitimate impediment, not simply and solely to the *celebration*, but also to the *application* of Mass for the people.

Before examining the excusing causes themselves it is important to note the relation between the personal and temporal elements. The general rule contained in the Code is:

1. the one bound by the obligation is to apply the Mass personally;

2. when he is legitimately impeded he must have the Mass applied on the canonical day by another;

3. when he cannot apply Mass himself, or have it applied by another on that day, he may transfer it to the following day if it can be said then.

This gradation evidently stresses the personal obligation. Only when the one bound is legitimately hindered from applying Mass himself for the people may he have another apply it for him. Yet the temporal element prevails over the personal in this sense,

---

[4] *Commentary*, II, 363.

[5] *Institutiones*, I, n. 397, footnote 3.

[6] ". . . si ab eius celebratione quacumque coniungitur personalis applicatio."—Blat, *Commentarium*, II, n. 363.

"To be legitimately hindered does not necessarily mean to be unable to say Mass at all, but only to apply Mass."—Kaiser, "Ecclesiastical Legislation on the Missa Pro Populo."—*ER*, LXI (1919), 366.

"If then a pastor finds himself unable to apply (not merely to celebrate), for his people, he is obliged *ex justitia* to have another priest to say it for him . . ."—*Ibidem*, p. 425.

[7] C. 419.

that if the subject is impeded from satisfying both the personal and temporal elements of the obligation simultaneously, his duty is to give preference to the temporal and to see that the Mass is applied on the day assigned by another priest; and only if that is impossible is he justified in deferring the application of the Mass and even then he is bound to apply the Mass as soon as possible, either personally or by proxy. This is expressly stated with regard to bishops; it is legitimately inferred with regard to pastors, since canon 466, §1 says that pastors are to apply Mass for the people according to the norms of canon 339. One point to be noted is that when the subject is so excused that he can neither apply Mass himself for his people, nor have the Mass applied by some one else on the day assigned, the law leaves him free to apply Mass personally or by proxy on the following day. It does not insist on the personal element when the obligation is postponed.

B. *Legitimate Impediments According to Canon 339.* What causes constitute legitimate impediments to the personal celebration of the Mass for the people on the days assigned?

1. *Sickness,* preventing one from celebrating Mass, is a legitimate impediment which would justify the one bound in having Mass applied for the people by another; it would in fact oblige him to do so.

2. *Irregularity,* because of which he would be forbidden to celebrate Mass, would place him under an obligation of having Mass applied for the people by some one else on the same day.[8]

3. *Legitimate absence* is a circumstance which would leave the subject free either to apply Mass for the people himself or have it applied by the priest who takes his place. This alternative choice is not extended to bishops since there is no obligation upon the bishop to apply the Mass for the people in any particular place.

4. *The obligation of celebrating a conventual Mass.* One bound to the obligation of a conventual Mass and Mass for the people on the same day may apply the Mass for the people through a proxy on the same day, or personally on the following day.[9] The words

---

[8] De Meester, *Compendium,* II, n. 846, b.

[9] "Si quis eodem die urgeatur onere utriusque Missae et pro populo et

of Canon 419, 2 leave a free choice of these alternatives. However the use of the proxy on the same day if possible seems more in accord with the spirit of the law.[10]

5. *Participation in a retreat,* the circumstances of which leave no opportunity to say Mass.[11] Under such circumstances one is bound to have Mass applied by a proxy on the day designated. If all the priests of a diocese were on retreat at the same time it seems that it would be permissible to postpone the application until one would be able to apply the Mass for the people himself.[12]

These causes certainly constitute legitimate impediments to the personal application of Mass for the people. There are other causes whose validity as legitimate impediments has been controverted. The following causes have been declared by pre-Code decisions of the Sacred Congregation of the Council as insufficient to constitute a just cause which would excuse from the obligation of personally applying Mass for the people.

1. *Contrary Custom.* In 1847 the Sacred Congregation was asked what must be thought of a custom in virtue of which a pastor on Sundays and feast-days applied a private Mass for a benefactor, and though bound by no legitimate impediment, transferred the burden of applying Mass for the people to another priest. The answer was " Consuetudinem, de qua agitur, non esse attendendam." [13] Again, in 1856, in answer to a request for an opinion regarding a custom by which all priests laboring in a parish took turns at applying Mass for the people, the Sacred Congregation answered that the burden of the application of Mass for the people belongs to the pastor.[14]

2. *A funeral Mass.* A negative answer was given to both parts of a question which asked whether pastors can celebrate the Mass

---

conventuali, hanc ipse celebret applicetque per se, illam per alium vel per se die sequenti."—C. 419, §2.

[10] Cf. *Supra*, p. 93.

[11] Chelodi, *Jus de Personis,* n. 227.

[12] *ER,* LIX (1918), 305.

[13] S. C. C., *Mechlinien,* 25 sept., 1847—Lucidi, *De Visitatione Sacrorum Liminum* (3 ed., 3 vols., Romae, 1883), n. 373.

[14] S. C. C., *Palicastren,* 23 maii, 1856—Lucidi, *De Visitatione Sacrorum Liminum,* n. 375.

for the dead on Sundays and other feast-days, the body being present, and transfer the application of the Mass for the people to another day; and if the answer to that query were negative, whether they could at least supply the application of the Mass for the people through another priest.[15] The order in which the question was put indicates the precedence of the temporal nature and the personal nature of the obligation. The Mass is to be celebrated on the day assigned, through the subject of the obligation, if possible, or through a proxy.

3. *A Nuptial Mass.*[16] It excuses from neither the personal nor the temporal obligation.

4. *A founded Mass,* when scheduled for a day on which there exists an obligation of applying Mass for the people. It does not offer a relaxation of either the personal or the temporal obligation.[17]

5. *The misconception of the faithful in attendance.* In this case the latter thought that the High Mass was applied for them, and therefore attended it. The Sacred Congregation not only declared that this is an insufficient cause for the pastor to transfer the obligation, but also declared that it was not expedient that the favor of following this custom be granted.[18]

6. *A Mass for a pious benefactor.*[19]

There is some question, however, as to whether or not these pre-Code responses, or at least whether some of them, are still in force; that is, whether they are to furnish the norm for interpreting the phrase, " legitime impediatur." De Meester declares that regard must be paid to these responses and because of them he holds these causes as insufficient to create a legitimate impediment: a funeral or a nuptial Mass, Mass for the fulfillment of a particular legacy, Mass at which the people assist under the impression that it is offered for them, contrary custom, lack of an

[15] S. C. C., *Fesulana* 27 ian. 1771—*Thesaurus Resolutionum,* XXXX, 1.

[16] S. C. C., *Castri Albi,* 18 iulii, 1789—*Thesaurus Resolutionum,* LXVIII, 147.

[17] S. C. C., *Melvitana,* 9 aprilis 1892—*ASS,* XXIV, 669.

[18] S. C. C. (without indication of diocese), 19 april, 1881—*ASS,* XIV, 332.

[19] S. C. C. Mechlinien, 25 sept. 1847, ad IV—*Nouvelle Revue Theologique,* XXVIII, 569.

adequate income.[20] This conclusion seemed certain regarding Sundays and feasts. He feels that this question even under the present law must be solved in the same way.[21] This view is also held by Noldin,[22] Cocchi,[23] and Marc-Gestermann,[24] who quote the causes hitherto mentioned and say that they have been declared insufficient by the Sacred Congregation of the Council. Cappello mentions the causes declared insufficient by the Sacred Congregation and states that according to the norms of canons 6, 2° and 4°, and 23, it must certainly be held that these declarations still have force. He mentions as an additional argument for their binding force today, the fact that the obligation of the application of Mass for the people is of divine-ecclesiastical law and these declarations explain the implications of not merely ecclesiastical law, but also the divine law itself. Further the divine law obviously *per se* imposes an obligation that is personal because the sacerdotal office of mediator which is exercised through the applying of the sacrifice is a personal obligation. From this it follows, says Cappello, that the pastor who can indeed fulfill other duties through another cannot habitually satisfy the obligation of Mass for the people through another. It was in determining the degree in which a pastor could so satisfy his obligation that the declarations were issued. They are not therefore limited to the interpretation of ecclesiastical law.[25]

Koudelka also feels that the pre-Code responses furnish the norm. " What is meant by a ' legitimate impediment ' here? Are we to interpret this term acccording to the old law? It seems that there is no other way possible. The term is of frequent occurrence in the old law in connection with this point, and so it would seem but natural that the legislators meant to use it in the same signification as it had there. This is the more true since no further explanation has been given it in the new law itself." [26]

---

[20] De Meester, *Compendium,* II, n. 846.

[21] De Meester, *Compendium,* II, n. 847.

[22] *De Sacramentis,* n. 184, b.

[23] *Commentarium,* III, n. 346, d.

[24] *Institutiones Morales Alphonsianae,* n. 1606, 3°.

[25] Cappello, *De Sacramentis,* I, n. 650.

[26] Koudelka, *Pastors, Their Rights and Duties,* p. 50.

Vermeersch, however, in affirming that a funeral Mass could be a legitimate impediment, holds that the pre-Code response denying this need not be taken as a norm for interpreting the term "legitime impediatur." He holds that if one examines the proper force of this response he finds that the argument from canon 6, 2° is of little efficacy. The Sacred Congregation merely decided that the necessity of celebrating a funeral Mass did not suffice as an impediment. But such a decision or judgment depends on circumstances that can vary, so that today the cause arising from the necessity of celebrating a funeral Mass could be much more grave than it was considered in 1770 and 1771. The Code explicitly states that the obligation of a conventual Mass prevails over the obligation of Mass for the people; it can easily happen that in a certain place or for certain funerals, the personal celebration of such funerals is of greater urgency than the personal celebration of a conventual Mass. So Vermeersch argues that it can happen that the substitution of another priest in the place of the pastor for funeral services, in a given place or age, would be borne with equanimity by the parishioners, while in another age or place it would seriously offend them. As an additional argument he mentions that though the IV Provincial Council of Mechlin in 1920 indicated as legitimate impediment excusing from the personal celebration of Mass for the people, funerals or other solemn offices which could not be deferred, its acts were approved by the Holy See. Hence, says Vermeersch, one must distinguish between responses which absolutely interpret the law as such, and responses which contain an application of the law to a changeable fact.[27]

Notwithstanding Vermeersch, the correct view is that these decisions are still in force. According to canon 6, 2° canons which restate the former law in its entirety must be interpreted in accordance with the old law. According to number 3 of the same canon, canons which agree only in part with the old law, in what they agree are to be interpreted according to the old law; further according to number 4, in a case of doubt as to whether some provision of the canons differs from the old law, one must adhere to

[27] Vermeersch, "De canone 466 et de recta applicatione can. 6, §2."—*Periodica*, XVII (1928), 136*–138*.

the old law. The papal documents on the application of Mass for the people did not treat this particular question of legitimate excuse. The pre-Code law on this matter was that of the responses of the Sacred Congregation. The Sacred Congregation was asked on several occasions whether certain causes were legitimate impediments which would justify one bound by the obligation of the application of Mass for the people in having this Mass said by another on the day appointed, or, as was asked in some cases, in postponing the application to another day. It answered that these causes were not sufficient. The Code does not depart from that law on this question. It merely says that if the bishop is legitimately impeded from personally applying Mass for the people on the days appointed, he should apply Mass through another on those days. Therefore, the old law admitting or rejecting situations as legitimate impediments still holds, since it is not opposed to the precepts of the Code. The phrase, " legitime impediens " is substantially the old law and is therefore to be interpreted according to the old law.

Cappello is correct in his opinion. But his additional argument, namely that these declarations explain the implications of not merely ecclesiastical law but also the divine law itself is not acceptable. The obligation of the application of Mass for the people is admittedly of divine law. But its determination is by canon law. If the Sacred Congregation of the Council were to decide that any or all of these causes constituted legitimate impediments, the decision would be valid and there would be no derogation from the divine law.

The reason already adduced why these decisions of the Sacred Congregation are still in force may be briefly summarized as this:

1. they constitute the pre-Code law; 2. the Code retains the discipline of the old law, restating it in general terms; 3. therefore the old law in this matter remains in the Code and with it the declarations of the Sacred Congregation.

Vermeersch's argument that the decision of the Sacred Congregation regarding the insufficiency of the funeral Mass as a legitimate impediment was merely based on circumstances which are no longer in effect is a gratuitous assertion. Had the Holy See wished to change the law in the light of changed circumstances, it might have done so in the Code. Instead it simply said that a legitimate impediment was necessary, without saying anything new of the nature of that impediment. As a concession the Code gave to the bishop the faculty of permitting the postponement for a just cause. Further the Commission for the Interpretation of the Code is authorized to declare whether there has been a change in the nature of the causes sufficient to constitute a legitimate impediment to the personal application of Mass for the people. It has not done so. Hence there is no ground for assuming that due to a change in circumstances upon which it was based, the response given under the old law is no longer in force.

It is true that a local council held since the Code has declared that such cases are sufficient as legitimate impediments to the personal application of the Mass for the people. It is also true that the Acts of this Council have been approved by the Holy See. Yet these facts do not militate against the binding force of previous declarations that such causes were insufficient to constitute legitimate impediments. Canon 466, §3 gives the Ordinary of the place the right to permit a pastor for a just cause to apply Mass for the people on another day from that on which he is bound by law. If several Ordinaries exercise this power and grant this permission through the medium of a council they are acting within their rights and do nothing to lessen the binding force of the pre-Code decisions. They are saying, in effect, " These are the just causes for which, in virtue of the power given us in canon 466 we permit you to postpone the obligation of the application of Mass for the people." They are not saying, " These are the causes which constitute you legitimately impeded in the sense of canon 339."

While the correctness of their view is not admitted the authority of such authors as Vermeersch,[28] Coronata,[29] and Augustine [30] is

---

[28] *Epitome*, I, n. 553, 2; cfr. also *Periodica*, XXVII, 136.

[29] "si legitime impediatur . . . Augustine II, 363, interpretatur de impedimento non ad dicendam Missam absolute, sed ad dicendam Missam pro populo, quia, e. g. ea die celebrare debet pro speciale intentione, pro funere, pro sponsis, pro pinguiori stipendio: quae interpretatio probabilis videtur."—Coronata, *Institutiones*, I, n. 397, footnote 3.

[30] ". . . si ab eius celebratione legitime impediatur does not mean that a bishop is unable to say Mass at all, but that he is not able to apply his Mass; for instance, he may have to say a Mass for a special intention, a

in favor of the notion that legitimate impediments to the personal application of the Mass for the people are the following: a funeral Mass, a nuptial Mass, application of anniversary Mass for parents, a large stipend for a Mass to be applied for a special intention on the day of obligation. Kaiser also holds that these causes constitute legitimate impediments, but he adds that while they would be legitimate impediments permitting a pastor or bishop to have Mass applied for the people by another on the day appointed, they would not justify a pastor in applying Mass for the people personally on another day without the permission of the Ordinary.[31] Woywood makes an exception in the case of a pastor who is the only priest in the parish and who has to say a funeral or nuptial Mass on a holy day.[32] He holds that such a one may say those Masses and postpone the application of Mass for the people to another day; for one may reasonably hold that the law of the Code does not intend to interfere with his parish work. However, this statement regarding the non-interference of the Code with parish work cannot be adduced as an argument. The Code regulates by direct provision the work of a pastor. When it places an obligation upon him that is part of the parish work according to canonical regulation. That obligation is not to be removed simply on the assumption that its presence constitutes an unforeseen interference with another phase of his pastoral work, particularly in view of the fact that the Code in canon 466, §3 provides that the bishop may permit such a transfer for a just cause.

In favor of the opinion that, because of the pre-Code decisions of the Sacred Congregation of the Council, those causes do not constitute a legitimate impediment to the personal application of

---

funeral Mass, or a *Missa pro sponso et sponsa,* or perhaps he has a *pingue stipendium* for that day and no other. All these and similar reasons are considered lawful, provided a bishop complies with the rest of the canon." —Augustine, *Commentary,* II, 363.

". . . of course, any legitimate cause (e. g. sickness, some other personal duty, application of the Mass for his parents *in die obitus seu anniversarii,* or for a public cause) would justify him in having the Mass for the people said by another."—Augustine, *Commentary,* II, 550.

31 Kaiser, "Ecclesiastical Legislation on the Missa pro Populo."—*ER,* LXI (1919), 366.

32 *HPR,* XXXI (1939–1931), 297.

the Mass for the people are: De Meester,[33] Wernz-Vidal,[34] Cappello,[35] Cocchi,[36] Noldin,[37] Koudelka,[38] Marc-Gastermann-Rauss,[39] O'Neil,[40], and Aertnys-Damen.[41] What then is to be the attitude of one bound by the obligation, who is faced with a request to celebrate, or the necessity of satisfying the obligation of celebrating a Mass for another intention on the day on which he is bound to apply Mass for the people? He is bound to secure the permission of his Ordinary. He might, however, take advantage of the opinion which holds that these reasons would legitimately impede him from the application of Mass for the people, on the grounds that the authority of Vermeersch, Coronata and Augustine make that opinion at least probable.[42]

C. *Just Cause—According to Canon 466.* However, though a bishop might take advantage of the latter opinion, for a pastor to act in accordance with it seems a subterfuge in view of the fact that the Code grants to the local Ordinary the faculty of permitting the transfer of the application of Mass for the people to another day. In other words the Code foresees the possibility of some impediment to the application of Mass for the people by the pastor on a particular day, one perhaps not recognized before the Code by the Sacred Congregation of the Council, and makes provision for such cases in paragraph three of canon 466.[43]

The local Ordinary can, for a just cause, permit a pastor to apply Mass for the people on a day other than that to which the obligation is attached by law. De Meester seems to hold that this just cause is to be interpreted according to the pre-Code procedure.

---

[33] *Compendium*, II, n. 846.
[34] *Ius Canonicum*, IV[1], n. 76.
[35] *De Sacramentis*, I, n. 650.
[36] *Commentarium*, III, n. 346.
[37] *De Sacramentis*, n. 184, b.
[38] *Pastors*, p. 50.
[39] *Institutiones Morales Alphonsianae*, n. 1606.
[40] O'Neil, *Irish Ecclesiastical Record*, XL (1932), 406.
[41] *Theologia Moralis*, n. 1146, 2.
[42] Cf. C. 15.
[43] Cf. Motry, *ER*, XCII (1935), 299.

Before the Code the Ordinary did not have the faculty now given him by the Code. Some Ordinaries did obtain it at times by a special indult. De Meester interprets " justa de causa " in the light of the causes enumerated in these indults as justifying the permission to transfer the application of the Mass for the people, e. g., a funeral Mass or nuptial Mass, which cannot be anticipated or transferred, provided there is no priest to whom the application of Mass for the people can conveniently be transferred on the day of obligation; or, in the case of a poor pastor who is forced to depend on the Mass stipends for his livelihood, a small income. Hence De Meester rejects the opinion holding as just causes for the Ordinary to intervene, founded Masses, a third, seventh or thirtieth day Mass, an anniversary Mass, or a manual Mass for an urgent cause. He argues that this opinion is too alien to the practice of the Roman Curia to be upheld, though he notes that Cocchi and Cappello propose it.[44]

However there seems to be no good reason why the words " justa de causa " in this canon should be interpreted in a restrictive sense. Interpretation is primarily to be made according to the proper signification of the words taken in text and context; and if the latter then remain doubtful, resort is to be had to parallel cases in the Code. Since this faculty given to the Ordinary to permit the transfer for a just cause is a new thing in the law, there is no reason to interpret that phrase as being restricted by pre-Code practice.[45] A further reason, cited by some authors, is that the particular restrictive concessions, given by the Sacred Congregation of the Council before the Code, are not to be regarded as applicable since they are not listed as sources of the canon.[46] This is not a valid argument since the footnotes of the Code, as foot-

---

[44] *Compendium*, II, n. 847, d.

[45] "Facultas haec Ordinariis olim per indultum concedebatur, cum Codex eam iuris communis faciat, latam interpretationem patitur."—Vermeersch-Creusen *Epitome*, I, n. 553.

[46] Brys, "De Celebratione Pro Grege."—*Collationes Burgensis*, XXVIII (1928), 460–470;

Claeys-Bouuaert, " Quid statuatur per ius tum commune, tum particulare nostrum, circa obligationem parochorum missam celebrandi pro populo."—*Collationes Gandavenses*, XII (1925), 174–180.

notes, are not norms of interpretation, and have no official authority.

In response to De Meester's statement that the opinion holding that a just cause is not only a funeral or nuptial Mass, but also a founded Mass, or a third, seventh or thirtieth day Mass, an anniversary Mass, or a manual Mass for an urgent cause, is too contrary to the practice of the Roman See to be tenable, Cappello states confidently that this opinion is, on the contrary, fully in accord with the practice of the Sacred Congregation of the Council and that he proposes it as the surer opinion, and as the more secure.[47]

The fact remains that there is no reason to restrict the meaning of "justa de causa" in this canon any more than in other canons of the Code; therefore the cause required need merely be just and reasonable, its gravity being proportionate to the gravity of the law.[48] Hence the cause may be extrinsic or intrinsic to the law; for the common good or a private interest; it can be merely a difficulty in observing the law in a particular case, or the good will of the superior; and of course it need not be grave enough to excuse from the law, of itself.[49] Therefore, examples of a just cause, for which the Ordinary of the place can permit a pastor to apply Mass for the people on a day other than that on which he is bound by law are:

a. a funeral or a nuptial Mass that cannot be transferred to another day;[50]

b. the inadequacy of the income of a pastor who is forced to depend on Mass stipends for his livelihood;[51]

---

[47] Cappello, "Esame di alcune opere di diritto e di teologia morale."—*Gregorianum,* VI (1925), 295.

[48] C. 84, §1.

[49] Van Hove, *De Rescriptis,* vol. I, tom. IV, n. 455; Coronata, *Institutiones,* I, n. 114.

[50] Chelodi, *Ius de Personis,* n. 227, footnote 4; Beste, *Introductio in Codicem,* p. 295; Prummer, *Theologia Moralis,* III, n. 258, a; Cappello, *Summa,* I, n. 529, 4º.

[51] Chelodi, *op. cit.,* n. 227; Beste, *op. cit.,* p. 295; Sipos, *Enchiridion Iuris Canonici,* p. 319.

c. founded Masses, which by foundation are scheduled for the day on which one is bound to apply Mass for the people;[52]

d. a third, seventh, or thirtieth day Mass;[53]

e. an anniversary Mass;[54]

f. a Gregorian Mass;[55]

g. spiritual exercises, e. g. a retreat, which prevent the celebration of Mass on the day of obligation;[56]

h. a manual Mass for an urgent cause.[57]

Is it necessary for the pastor to seek the permission of the Ordinary in each single case? The law itself makes no statement on this point. It is generally agreed that the permission of the Ordinary is not required for one act, or else that it may be presumed for a single case.[58] O'Neil alone objects to this notion, saying, "Wernz-Vidal thinks that the express permission of the bishop may not be required for a single case, but only for its repeated transference in given circumstances. We do not know on what principle this position could be maintained, unless it be an appeal to *epikeia,* and even *epikeia* may not be invoked when the superior

---

[52] Cappello, *De Sacramentis,* I, n. 652.

[53] Cappello, *loc. cit.*

[54] Cappello, *loc. cit.*

[55] Cappello, *loc. cit.;* Chelodi, *Ius de personis,* n. 227; Toso, *Commentaria Minora,* C. 466, n. 4; Cocchi, *Commentarium,* II, n. 346, b.

[56] Chelodi, *Ius de Personis,* n. 227; Toso, *loc. cit.; ER,* CV (1941), 305.

[57] Cappello, *De Sacramentis,* I, n. 652.

[58] "Licentia Ordinarii praesumi potest si de actu unico agatur." Coronata, *Institutiones,* I, n. 484, c. footnote 5.

"Censemus expressam Ordinarii licentiam non requiri ad unum vel alterum actum."—Cappello, *Summa,* n. 529, 4°;

"Expressa licentia episcopi ad unum actum non videtur esse stricte necessaria sed solum ut mutatio diei fieri possit permanenti modo quoties illa causa occurenti."—Chelodi, *Ius de Personis,* n. 227, footnote 4.

"In casu particulari licentia etiam praesumi potest."—Beste, *Introductio in Codicem,* p. 295.

"Illa expressa licentia Episcopi ad unum actum non videtur videtur esse stricte necessaria, sed solum ut mutatio diei fieri possit permanenti modo quoties illa causa occurrerit."—Wernz-Vidal, *Ius Canonicum,* II, n. 736, III, c. footnote 1;

"Dispensatio autem ad actum, iusta causa intercedente, semper praesumi posse videtur."—Toso, *Commentaria Minora,* C. 466.

may be approached." [59] It is correct to say that the permission of the Ordinary may be presumed in a single case. The cause usually arises suddenly with little opportunity to approach the bishop. Indeed it can even be held that a dispensation is tacitly granted; for it is not unusual for pastors to act on a presumed permission to transfer the application of the Mass for the people in a particular case. The fact that the bishop does not prohibit this when he could easily do so affords grounds for supposing that a tacit dispensation has been granted for the particular case.

D. *Exercise of the Dispensing Power of Canon 466.* It has been established that the permission of the Ordinary may be presumed in a single case, so that for just cause the pastor might transfer the application of Mass for the people to a day other than that decreed in the law. But while this holds for a single case, what of a pastor who habitually avails himself of this presumed permission, or of the opinion that permission is not required for a single act? It might be maintained that he is considering each case as it occurs, that in each instance he is presuming the permission of the Ordinary for one case, and that by this means he is remaining within the bounds laid down by the authors, since his manner of acting does not constitute what Wernz-Vidal and Chelodi call a change of the day of obligation in a permanent manner effective as often as the given cause occurs.[60] Yet this is precisely what such a practice amounts to and it goes beyond the bounds of the " single act " for which authors do not require the permission of the Ordinary.

Some Ordinaries have taken a means of relieving their pastors of this difficulty by granting them the faculty for just cause of applying Mass for the people on a day other than that which the law prescribes. This is legitimate and particularly in accord with the spirit of the law when the just causes listed by the Ordinary are such that they contribute primarily to the benefit of the parishioners rather than the pastor. Examples of such statutes are

---

[59] O'Neil, *Irish Ecclesiastical Record,* XL (1932), 406.

[60] Chelodi, *Ius de Personis,* n. 227; Wernz-Vidal, *Ius Canonicum,* II, n. 736, footnote 1.

found in the Acts and Decrees of the IV Provincial Council of Portland in Oregon, and the IV Council of Mechlin.[61]

The Portland Council announces that it is granted to pastors in their faculties that for just cause they may apply Mass for the people on a day other than that which is decreed in the law. A just cause, it states, is a funeral Mass or a nuptial Mass. The Belgian Council permits, when two conditions are fulfilled, the pastor to transfer the Mass to another priest on the same day, or, if that is not possible, to say it on another day personally or by proxy. The conditions are, first, that the impeding cause is one that cannot be deferred, second, that the cause be a funeral Mass or other solemn office, or that he be legitimately impeded in another way such as by sickness. Belgian commentators say that examples of the solemn office are the nuptial Mass, anniversary requiem Mass, a memorial Mass, or a Mass of Thanksgiving for a public event, for example the Mass which is held in many places on Armistice Day. They note however that if it is a question of a manual Mass or some other non-solemn office, it is a case for a special recourse to the bishop.[62]

The noteworthy thing about these statutes is that they relieve the pastor from either presuming the permission or of recurring to the Ordinary in the two very common cases of a nuptial or funeral Mass which he cannot defer to a day not dedicated to the application of Mass for the people. Yet they make it clear that he must

---

[61] "In pagella facultatum conceditur parochis ut possint iusta de causa applicare Missam pro populo alia die ab ea quae iure statuitur; iusta autem causa censetur Missae exsequialis vel Missa pro nupturientibus. Missa translata applicetur prima die libera."—*Acta et Decreta Concilii Provincialis Portlandensis in Oregon Quarti* (Sentinel Printery, Portland, Oregon, 1934), Decretum 137;

". . . quodsi exsequias defuncti aut aliud solemne officium quod differri non possit peragendum ipse (parochus) habeat, vel alio modo, v. g. ratione infirmitatis legitime impediatur, statis diebus applicet per alium; si neque id praestare possit, quamprimum per alium applicet alia die."—Fourth Council of Mechlin, decretum 150 (as quoted in the *Collationes Brugensis,* t. XXVIII, 465).

[62] Brys, "De Celebratione pro grege."—*Collationes Bruensis,* XXVIII (1928), 465; Claeys-Bouuaert, "Quid statuatur . . . circa obligationem parochorum missam celebrandi pro populo."—*Collationes Gandavenses,* XII (1925), 172–173.

recur in cases of a less public nature, notably that he might say a manual Mass for a stipend.[63]

The most recent example of the exercise of the power given the Ordinary in canon 466 is contained in the Formula of faculties granted to the priests of the Archdiocese of New York Feb. 11, 1942. The Archbishop grants to those of his priests who have the obligation of applying Mass for the people the faculty of transferring this Mass to another day, if they are impeded by a just cause from applying on the day decreed. He imposes the restriction, however, that this Mass is not to be postponed beyond the fifth day.[64]

Note that the Belgian Council as to preference to be exercised in the process of transfer expressly applies to pastors what canon 339, §4 decrees directly of bishops, namely, that the temporal character prevails over the personal so that the impeded or excused pastor is authorized first to have the Mass said on the day of obligation by another priest, and, only if this is not possible, to defer the application to another day. This is completely in accord with the Code. For while canon 466, §4 makes no provision for the Ordinary to permit the pastor to transfer the obligation to another priest, but only to transfer the application of the Mass by himself to another day, any cause which would justify the applying of Mass for the people on a day other than the day of obligation, with greater certainty would justify the applying of the Mass by another priest on the proper day.

E. *Causes Excusing from the Local Obligation.* C. 466, 4.—Parochus Missam pro populo applicandem celebret in ecclesia

[63] "But in the knowledge of the writer there is no statement of any author, and no statute of any diocesan synod that allows the pastor regularly to transfer the application of the *Missa pro populo* to make room for the celebration of a high Mass for its attached stipend in view of some private intention."—Anonymous, "The Missa Pro Populo"—*ER*, CV (1941), 305.

[64] "Formula Facultatum Quae Sacerdotibus Dioeceseos Neo-Eboracenses concedi solent, I, 'Transferendi in aliam diem, non ultra tamen quintam, applicationem Missae pro populo, si hac obligatione oneretur et iusta causa impediatur ne die statuta applicet.'"—*Conference Bulletin of the Archdiocese of New York,* XIX (1942), 35.

paroeciali, nisi rerum adiuncta Missam alibi celebrandam exigant aut suadeant.

5.—Legitime absens parochus potest Missam pro populo applicare vel ipse per se in loco in quo degit, vel per sacerdotem qui eius vices gerat in paroecia.

The local character of the application of Mass for the people does not extend to bishops or those burdened as bishops in the law by this obligation, but only to pastors and those burdened as pastors in law by this obligation. The legislation of the Code in this respect is a reflection of the preceding law. " The reasons which oblige a parish priest are different from those which oblige a bishop. For as to each parish priest is committed a special and definite care of the people in a parish he must not only celebrate for the people on festal days but also admit them to the parochial church to assist at Mass. . . . Now the same reasons do not hold for bishops who are placed in a different relation to the multitude; for by no law are bishops bound at the present day to offer the Holy Sacrifice in their Cathedrals on Sundays and holidays."[65] From these words of Pope Leo it is evident that Bishops, Vicars Capitular, and Apostolic Administrators are not bound to apply the Mass for the people in the Cathedral church, nor are Abbots or Prelates Nullius bound to apply in the church of the place in which they rule. But by the same papal provision pastors are bound to the local church in the discharge of this burden, and what is said of them applies also to quasi-pastors, and parochial administrators if they enjoy full parochial rights. The legislation of Pope Leo XIII is reflected in the canon of the Code which prescribes that the pastor is to apply Mass for the people in the parish church. That is the rule. The canon itself states, in broad and general terms, the possibility of exceptions to that rule. It allows the pastor to celebrate elsewhere the Mass applied for the people, when circumstances either demand or advise it. It is left to the prudent judgment of the pastor to decide when the general terms of the canon " adiuncta " and " suadeant " are verified. A cause less grave than is necessary for excuse from the personal or tem-

[65] Leo XIII const. " In suprema," 9 iunii, 1882—*Fontes,* n. 585, translated by Wiseman, *The Pastor,* III (1884), 371.

poral obligation would excuse from the local obligation, and in this case the permission of the Ordinary is not required. Hence authors enumerate many causes which would excuse: attendance of parishioners in great numbers at some pilgrimage church, the ceremonies of first communion carried out at some particular shrine, the greater convenience of the faithful in assisting at Mass elsewhere than in the parochial church, the use of a winter chapel or schoolhouse, necessity of celebrating Mass outside the church because of the repairing of the parish church, the personal infirmity of the pastor preventing his going to the parish church, and the existence of a local interdict resting on the parish church.[66]

ARTICLE II. RIGHTS AND OBLIGATIONS OF THE SUBSTITUTE

From the foregoing cases it is evident that there will be more than a few instances in which the one bound by the obligation of applying Mass for the people, be he priest or bishop, will licitly have the Mass applied by another. In that case, for the priest applying the Mass it becomes a manual Mass for which he is entitled to a stipend in justice. What is to be the amount of this offering? He who transmits a manual stipend to others ought to pass on the whole amount he received.[67]

Would a pastor then be bound to compute the difference between his salary and that of an assistant and thus decide what is the offering due in justice to another priest each time the latter satisfies the pastor's obligation of applying Mass for the people? No, for it is not correct to maintain that the additional salary is given solely in view of the more than eighty Masses the pastor is obliged to apply for the people during the year. The diocesan tax defines the amount of the stipend of the Mass for the people whenever it is said.[68]

---

[66] Blat, *Commentarium*, II, n. 513; De Meester, *Compendium*, II, n. 848; Augustine, *Commentary*, II, 551; Toso, *Commentaria Minora*, C. 466; Cappello, *De Sacramentis*, n. 651; Cocchi, *Commentarium*, III, n. 346, c.

[67] C. 840, §1.

[68] "A pastor need give only a manual stipend to the curate for saying the Missa pro Populo, because the income of the benefice is intended to be the salary for the pastor's whole sustenance, not merely to be the stipends for the Masses which he must say for his parishioners."—Keller, *Mass Stipends* (The Catholic University of America Canon Law Studies, No. 27,

Since the Mass for the people is a Mass to which the pastor is bound in justice, he is not permitted to accept a stipend for it, or when he binates, for either Mass. This restriction applies also to anyone else who is obliged to apply Mass for the people. It is occasionally argued that, in the case where a curate accepts the obligation on a particular day as a favor to a pastor, and without receiving any stipend for it, he is free to accept a stipend for the second Mass since he is under no obligation in justice to apply the Mass for the people. In other words there is no violation of canon 824, §2 since the curate is applying only one Mass, the Mass for the stipend, from a title of justice.[69] According to this view the pastor would then be free to receive a stipend for one Mass on the same day. Mahoney,[70] Schaaf,[71] and Keller,[72] oppose this view and say that such a procedure would be gravely unlawful. The people of the parish are entitled in justice to the application of Mass on that day. The authors just named feel that the curate, or other priest who is not pastor, in undertaking the application of Mass for the people even without a stipend, assumes a real obligation in justice toward the parish, even though his obligation toward the pastor on this account may technically be in charity or fidelity. By his act of charity he assumes the pastor's obligation and becomes bound under a title of justice, even as the pastor was bound.

It is exactly this last point that is the centre of the difficulty. How is the curate bound in justice to something he has offered to do in charity? It is not enough to say that since the Mass is due in justice, it must bind someone in justice. The pastor satisfies his obligation by having the Mass applied. (This is prescinding from

---

Washington, D. C.: The Catholic University of America, 1925), p. 142; cf. also *ER*, LXIII (1920), 292, and LXV (1921), 301; *Il Monitore Ecclesiastico, anno* LIV serie V (1929), 314.

[69] *ER*, XCIV (1936), 533; *The Clergy Review*, I (1931), 225.

[70] *The Clergy Review*, I (1931), 225.

[71] *ER*, XCIV (1936), 533.

[72] "A visitor . . . who celebrates two Masses on Sunday as a favor to the pastor is forbidden to take a stipend for either Mass if he applies the other as the Missa pro populo; but the pastor may accept a stipend on that Sunday because he has transferred to the visitor the obligation of applying the Missa pro populo ex justitia."—Keller, *Mass Stipends*, p. 45.

the fact of the legality of his failing to apply the Mass personally.) The opinion of Mahoney and Keller seems to be based on that fact that this is an evasion of the law and is opposed to the spirit of the law. In other words, it is a subterfuge to eliminate the *ex justitia* title requiring the application of Mass for the people by passing it to another. But the question is not concerned with the intentions of the pastor and curate, or with the possible illicitness of the transfer. It is concerned merely with whether or not the curate, in applying Mass for the people without accepting a stipend, and also, under the privilege of bination, offering another Mass for a stipend, is violating canon 824, §2, which prescribes that a priest who offers Mass twice in one day, if he applies one Mass under an obligation of justice, may not accept a stipend for the second Mass.

It has not been proved that when the curate applies Mass for the people without accepting a stipend for it he is offering it under an obligation of justice. Therefore he, as well as the pastor, would be free to offer a Mass for a stipend that day under those circumstances.

CONCLUSIONS

1. Before the Council of Trent there was no definite legislation of a universal character regarding the obligation of applying Mass for the people.

2. The root of the obligation of applying Mass for the people is founded in the possession of an office to which the care of souls is attached. The obligation therefore is based on a unilateral contract, binding not under strict commutative justice but by a grave obligation of the natural law, based on legal justice or the duty of an official to the spiritual society.

3. The obligation to apply Mass for the people committed to his care does not bind the subject of the obligation to include the deceased members of his flock.

4. Religious superiors are bound by an obligation deriving from divine, not from ecclesiastical law, to apply Mass for their subjects occasionally.

5. Military chaplains, serving in the armed forces of the United States, are not bound to apply Mass for the people.

6. The obligation binds even on suppressed feasts which were formerly of obligation in virtue of particular law.

7. In a year in which the feast of the Annunciation or the feast of a patron falls on Good Friday the obligation ceases for that day.

8. The feast of the patron of a diocese can come under the term " patron of a place," as to the existence of the obligation of applying Mass from the people, if the necessary conditions are observed in choosing the patron.

9. The pre-Code decisions of the Sacred Congregation of the Council regarding the insufficiency of certain causes to constitute legitimate impediments are in force in regard to the term " si legitime impediatur " of canon 339, §4.

10. " Si ab eius celebratione legitime impediatur " in canon 339, §4 does not mean merely that the subject is excused from his obligation only when unable to celebrate Mass at all but also when he is impeded from applying his Mass for the people.

11. The words "iusta de causa" of canon 466, §3 need not be interpreted in a restrictive sense, and just causes for which a bishop may permit the transfer of the application of Mass for the people are not only those causes enumerated in indults previously granted by the Holy See in conceding the faculty now given in the law.

BIBLIOGRAPHY

SOURCES

Acta Apostolicae Sedis, Commentarium Officiale, Romae, 1909–

Acta et Decreta Sacrorum Conciliorum Recentiorum, Collectio Lacensis, 7 vols., Friburgi Brisgoviae, 1870–1892.

Acta et Decreta Concilii Plenarii Baltimorensis Tertii, A. D. MDCCCLXXXIV, Baltimorae, John Murphy, 1886.

Acta Sanctae Sedis, 41 vols., Romae, 1865–1908.

AGUIRRE, JOSEPHUS SAENZ DE, *Collectio Maxima Conciliorum Omnium Hispaniae et Novi Orbis,* 4 vols., Romae, 1693–1694.

Annuario Pontificio per l'anno 1940, Città del Vaticano: Typografia Poliglotta Vaticana, 1940.

Biblictheca Patrum, 28 vols., Lugduni, 1667.

Bullarium Diplomatum et Privilegiorum Sanctorum Romanorum Pontificum Taurinensis Editio, 24 vols. et Appendix, Augustae Taurinorum-Neapoli, 1857–1872.

CABROL-LE CLERCQ, *Monumenta Ecclesiae Liturgica,* 6 vols., Parisiis, 1894.

Canones et Decreta Sacrosancti Oecumenici Concilii Tridentini, Romae, 1845.

Codicis Iuris Canonici Fontes cura Emi. Petri Card. Gasparri editi, 9 vols., Romae (postea Civitate Vaticana): Typis Polyglottis Vaticanis, 1923–1939. Vols. VII–IX ed. *cura et studio Emi. Iustiniani Card. Serédi.*

Collectanea S. Congregationis de Propaganda Fide, 2 vols., Romae: Typographia Poliglotta S. C. de Propaganda Fide, 1907.

Concilii Plenarii Baltimorensis II, in Ecclesia Metropolitana Baltimorensi a die VII ad diem XXI Octobris, A. D. MDCCCLXVI Habiti et a Sede Apostolica Recogniti, Acta et Decreta, 2 ed., Baltimorae, 1894.

Corpus Scriptorum Ecclesiasticorum Latinorum, Vindobonae, 1866–

HARDOUIN, JEAN, *Acta Conciliorum et Epistolae Decretales ac Constitutiones Summorum Pontificum,* 12 vols., Parisiis, 1715.

HAROLDUS, FRANCISCUS, *Lima Limata Conciliis, Constitutionibus Synodalibus et aliis Monumentis Quibus Ven. Alphonsus Mogroveius . . . Composuit,* Romae, 1673.

HARTZHEIM, JOSEPH, *Concilia Germaniae,* 11 vols., Coloniae Augustae Agrippinensium, 1759–1790.

JAFFE, *Regesta ab condita Ecclesia ad annum post Christum natum MCXCVIII, editionem secundam correctam et auctam auspiciis Gulielmi Quattenbach, curaverunt S. Löwenfeld, F. Kaltenbrunner, P. Ewald, Lipsiae,* 1885–1888.

Mansi, Joannes D., *Sacrorum Conciliorum Nova et Amplissima Collectio,* 53 vols. in 59, Parisiis, Arnhem, Lipsiae, 1901–1927.

Migne, Jacobus P., *Patrologiae Cursus Completus, Series Graeca,* 161 vols., Parisiis, 1856–1866.

————, Patrologiae Cursus Completus, Series Latina, 221 vols., Parisiis, 1844–1855.

Pallottini, S., *Collectio Omnium Conclusionum et Resolutionum Quae in Causis Propositis apud Sacram Congregationem Cardinalium S. Concilii Tridentini Interpretum Prodierunt ab eius Institutionem Anno MDLXIX ad Annum MDCCCLX, Distinctis Titulis Alphabetico Ordine per Materias digesta,* 17 vols., Romae, 1868–1893 (Appendix, vol. 18, 1895).

Societas Goerresiana, *Concilium Tridentinum, Diariorum, Actorum, Epistolarum, Tractatum Nova Collectio,* 13 tomes, Friburgi Brisgoviae, 1901–1938.

Thesaurus Resolutionum Sacrae Congregationis Concilii, 167 vols., Romae, 1718–1908.

Theiner, Augustinus, *Acta Authentica SS. Oecumenici Concilii Tridentini,* 2 vols., Zagrabiae, 1874.

Zamboni, *Collectio Declarationem Sacrae Congregationis Cardinalium Sacri Concilii Tridentini Interpretum,* 4 vols., Atrebati, 1860–1867.

REFERENCE WORKS

Aertnys, J.-Damen, C., *Theologia Moralis,* 13 ed., 2 vols., Taurini: Marietti, 1939.

(St.) Alphonsus Liguori, *Theologia Moralis,* Matriti, 1876.

————, *Homo Apostolicus,* Augustae Taurinorum, 1870.

Alvarez, *Algunos Testimonios Historicos Sobre la Misa "Pro Populo" ante del Concilio de Trento,* Camaguey, Cuba, 1931.

Arregui, A., *Summarium Theologiae Moralis,* 13 ed., Romae: Typis Pont. Universitatis Gregorianae, 1937.

Ayrinhac, H. A., *Constitution of the Church in the New Code of Canon Law,* New York: Longmans, 1930.

(Bachofen), Charles Augustine, *A Commentary on the New Code of Canon Law,* 8 vols., St. Louis: Herder & Co., 1925–1938. Vol. I, 6 ed., 1931; Vol. II, 6 ed., 1936; Vol. III, 5 ed., 1938; Vol. IV, 3 ed., 1925; Vol. V, 5 ed., 1935; Vol. VI, 3 ed., 1931; Vol. VII, 3 ed., 1930; Vol. VIII, 3 ed., 1931.

Babenstuber, L., *Ethica Supernaturalis Salisburgensis sive Cursus Theologiae Moralis,* Augustae Vindelicorum, 1718.

Barbosa, A., *Pastoralis Solicitudo sive de Officio et Potestate Parochi,* Lugduni, 1665.

————, *De Officio et Potestate Parochi,* Animadversiones et Additamenta, Ubaldo Giraldi, Romae, 1831.

BARGILLIAT, M., *Praelectiones Iuris Canonici,* 37 ed., Parisiis, 1923.

BERARDI, A., *De Parocho,* Faventiae, 1887.

BERENGO, J., *Enchiridion Parochorum,* 2 ed., Venetiis, 1877.

BESTE, U., *Introductio in Codicem,* Collegeville, Minnesota: St. John's Abbey Press, 1938.

BLAT, A., *Commentarium Textus Codicis Iuris Canonici,* 5 vols. in 7. Romae: Collegio "Anglico," 1921–1938. Vol. I, 1921; Vol. II, pars I, ed. altera, 1921; Vol. II, partes II et III, 3 ed., 1938; Vol. pars 1, 2 ed., 1924; Vol. III, partes II et III, 2 ed., 1934; Vol. IV, 1927; Vol. V, 1924.

BONA, J., *Opera Omnia,* Antwerpuae, 1723.

BONACINA, M., *Opera Omnia de Morali Theologia,* Lugduni, 1634.

BOUIX, D., *Tractatus de Parocho,* 3 ed., Parisiis, 1880.

BOUSCAREN, T. LINCOLN, *The Canon Law Digest,* Milwaukee: Bruce, 2 vols. and supplement, 1934, 1937 and 1941.

BUVEE, H., *Memento Pratique De Ministere Paroissial,* Parisiis, 1921.

CAPPELLO, F., *Tractatus Canonico-Moralis de Sacramentis,* Vol. I, *De Sacramentis in Genere, de Baptismo, Confirmatione, et Eucharistia,* 3 ed., Romae: Marietti, 1938.

————, *Summa Iuris Canonici,* ed. altera, Romae: Apud Aedes Universitatis Gregorianae, 1932–1936. Vol. I, 1932; Vol. II, 1934; Vol. III, 1936.

CICOGNANI, H., *Canon Law,* 2 ed. Authorized English version by J. M. O'Hara and F. Brennan, Philadelphia: Dolphin Press, 1935.

CHELODI, J., *Ius de Personis,* ed. altera, Tridentini: Libr. Edit. Tridentinum, 1927.

CLERICATUS, J., *Discordiae Forensis de Beneficiis atque Pensionibus,* Venetiis, 1707.

CLAEYS-BOUUAERT, F. et SIMENON, G., *Manuale Iuris Canonici,* vols. I et III. 4 ed.; vol. II, 2 ed., Ghent-Liege, 1934–1935.

CORONATA, MATTHAEUS CONTE, A, *Institutiones Iuris Canonici,* 5 vols. Taurini: Marietti, 1933–1939. Vols. I et II, 2 ed., 1939; Vol. III, 1933; Vol. IV, 1935; Vol. V, 1936.

COCCHI, G., *Commentarium in Codicem Iuris Canonici,* 8 vols., Taurinorum Augustae: Marietti, 1931–1940. Vol. I, 5 ed., 1938; Vol. II, 4 ed., 1937; Vol. III, 3 ed., 1931; Vol. IV, 3 ed., 1932; Vol. V, 3 ed., 1932; Vol. VI, 3 ed., 1933; Vol. VII, 3 ed., 1940; Vol. VIII, 4 ed., 1938.

DAVIS, H., *Moral and Pastoral Theology,* Heythrop Theological Series, II, 4 vols., New York: Sheed and Ward, 1935.

DE LUGO, J., *Disputationes Scholasticae et Morales,* Parisiis, 1769.

DE MEESTER, A., *Juris Canonici et Juris Canonico-Civilis Compendium,* nova ed., 3 vols. in 4, Brugis: Desclée, De Brouwer, 1921–1928.

DIANA, A., *R. P. D. Dianae Panormitani Clerici Regularis Episcoporum,* Venetiis, 1728.

ENGEL, L., *Collegium Universi Juris Canonici,* Beneventi, 1760.

ESCOBAR, A., *Summa Theologiae Moralis,* Lugduni, 1654.

Fagnanus, P., *Commentarium in Tertium Librum Decretalium*, Venetiis, 1709.

Fanfani, L., *De Iure Parochorum*, ed. altera, Taurini: Marietti, 1936.

Ferraris, L., *Prompta Bibliotheca, Canonica, Iuridica, Moralis, Theologica necnon Ascetica, Polemica, Rubristica, Historica*, 9 vols., Romae, 1885–1899.

Ferreres, J., *Compendium Theologiae Moralis*, 14 ed. (7 ed., post Codicem), 2 vols., Barcinone: Subirana, 1928.

Gasparri, P., *Tractatus Canonicus de Sanctissima Eucharistia*, 2 vols. Parisiis-Lugduni, 1897.

Gavantus, B., *Commentaria in Rubricas Missali*, Venetiis, 1774.

Genicot, E.-Salsmans, I., *Institutiones Theologiae Moralis*, 12 ed. (5 ed. post Codicem), 2 vols., Louvain: Museum Lessianum. 1931.

Hervé, J., *Manuale Theologiae Dogmaticae*, 4 vols., Parisiis: apud Berche et Pagis, 1935–1936. Vol. I, 16 ed., 1935; Vol. II, Vol. III, 15 ed., 1935; Vol. IV, 14 ed., 1936.

Hurtado, P., *De Residentia*, 2 vols., Lugduni, 1661.

Keller, C. F., *Mass Stipends*, The Catholic University of America Canon Law Studies, n. 27, Washington, D. C.: The Catholic University of America, 1925.

Kinsman, F. J., *Trent*, New York: Longmans, 1921.

Konings, A., *Commentarium in Facultates Apostolicas*, 4 ed. a Putzer, New York, 1897.

Koudelka, C. J., *Pastors, Their Rights and Duties*, The Catholic University of America Canon Law Studies, n. 11, Washington, D. C.: The Catholic University of America, 1921.

Lambertinus, P. (later Benedictus XIV), *Institutiones Ecclesiasticae*, 2 vols., Venetiis, 1789.

Layman, P., *Theologia Moralis*, Venetiis, 1719.

Lehmkuhl, A., *Theologia Moralis*, 2 vols., Friburgi Brisgoviae, 1884.

Lucidi, A., *De Visitatione Sacrorum Liminum*, 3 ed., 3 vols., Romae, 1883.

Marc-Gestermann-Raus, *Institutiones Morales Alphonsianae*, 18 ed., Lugduni: Typis Emmanuelis Vitte, 1927.

Merkelbach, B., *Summa Theologiae Moralis*, ed. altera, 3 vols., Parisiis, 1936.

Monacelli, *Formularium Legale, Practicum*, Romae, 1884.

Meier, C., *Penal Administrative Procedure Against Negligent Pastors*, The Catholic University of America Canon Law Series, No. 140, Washington, D. C.: The Catholic University of America, 1941.

Natalis, Alexander, *Historia Ecclesiastica Veteris Novique Testamenti*, Venetiis, 1719.

Noldin, H.-Schmitt, A., *Summa Theologiae Moralis*, 23–24 ed., 3 vols., Oeniponte: Rauch, 1935–1936.

Pasquiligo, D., *De Sacrificio Novae Legis Quaestiones Theologicae, Morales, Juridicae*, Venetiis, 1707.

Possevino, J. B., *Praxis Curae Pastoralis*, Coloniae Agripinae, 1645.

PRUMMER, D., *Manuale Theologiae Moralis,* 8 ed., 3 vols., Friburgi-Brisgoviae: Herder, 1936.

REIFFENSTUEL, A., *Jus Canonicum Universum,* 7 vols., Venetiis, 1735.

RENAUDOT, E., *Liturgiarum Orientalium Collectio,* 2 ed., 2 vols., Parisiis, 1847.

SABBETTI-BARRET, *Compendium Theologiae Moralis,* 27 ed., New York, 1919.

SALMANTICENSES, *Theologiae Moralis Cursus,* 6 vols. in 4, Venetiis, 1726.

SCHMALZGRUEBER, F., *Jus Ecclesiasticum Universum,* 5 tomes in 12 vols., Romae, 1843–1845.

SCOTUS, JOANNES DUNS, *Opera Omnia,* 26 vols., Parisiis, 1895.

SIPOS, S., *Enchiridion Iuris Canonici,* 3 ed., Pecs: Haladas, 1936.

SMITH, S. B., *Elements of Ecclesiastical Law,* 5 ed., 2 vols., New York, 1883.

SOTO, D., *De Justitia et Jure,* Venetiis, 1568.

SUAREZ, F., *Opera Omnia R. P. Francisci Suarezii,* 26 vols., Bruxellis et Parisiis: apud Ludovicum Vives, 1856–1861.

SYLVIUS, F., *Commentarium in Tertiam Partem S. Thomae Aquinatis,* Venetiis, 1726.

THOMAS AQUINAS, ST., *Doctoris Angelici Divi Thomae Aquinatis Opera Omnia,* 34 vols., Parisiis, apud Ludovicum Vives, 1871–1882.

TOSO, A., *Ad Codicem Iuris Canonici Commentaria Minora,* 5 vols., Romae: Marietti, 1920–1927.

VAN DER BERGE, *Institutiones Canonicae* (handwritten manuscript), undated.

VAN HOVE, A., *Commentarium Lovaniense in Codicem Iuris Canonici,* 1 vol. in 5 toms., Mechliniae-Romae: H. Dessain, 1928–1939. Tom. I, *Prolegomena,* 1928; Tom. II, *De Legibus Ecclesiasticis,* 1930; Tom. III, *De Consuetudine, De Temporis Supputatione,* 1933; Tom. IV, *De Rescriptis,* 1936; Tom. V, *De Privilegiis, De Dispensationibus,* 1939.

VASQUEZ, F., *Commentarium ac Disputationum in Tertiam Partem S. Thomae,* Lugduni, 1631.

VERHOEVEN, M., *Dissertatio Canonica de Sacrosancto Missae Sacrificio a Parochis Aliisque Curam Animarum Habentibus pro Plebe Sibi Concredita, Deo Offerendo Diebus Dominicis et Festis, etiam Indulto Apostolico die 9 Aprilis, 1802, in Universo Gallicanae Reipublicae Territorio Suppressis, Lovaniae,* 1842.

————, *De Praxi a Parochis Observanda in Celebratione Missae pro Populo,* Hasseleti, 1849.

VERMEERSCH, A., *Theologia Moralis,* 3 ed., 4 vols., Romae: Universita Gregoriana, 1933.

VERMEERSCH, A.-CREUSEN, I., *Epitome Iuris Canonici,* 3 vols., Mechlinae: H. Dessain, 1934–1937. Vol. I, 6 ed., 1937; Vol. II, 5 ed., 1934; Vol. III, 5 ed., 1936.

WERNZ, F.-VIDAL, P., *Ius Canonicum,* 7 tom. in 8 vols., Romae: apud Aedes Universitatis Gregorianae, 1927–1938. Tom. I, 1938; Tom. II, 2 ed.,

1928; Tom. III, 1933; Tom. IV, pars I, 1934; Tom. IV, pars II, 1935; Tom. V, 2 ed., 1928; Tom. VI, 1927; Tom. VII, 1937.

WOYWOD, S., *A Practical Commentary on the Code of Canon Law,* 5 ed., 2 vols., New York: Wagner, 1939.

PERIODICALS

Apollinaris, Romae, 1928–

Archiv für katholisches Kirchenrecht, Innsbruck, 1857–1861; Mainz, 1862–

Australasian Catholic Record, The, Manly, 1923–

Canoniste, Le, Paris, 1924–1926 (originally *Le Canoniste Contemporain,* Paris, 45 vols., 1878–1922).

Clergy Review, The, London, 1931–

Collationes Brugenses, Brugis Flandorum, 1896–

Collationes Gandavenses, Gandavi, 1909–

Correspondance de Rome, Liége, 1848–

Conference Bulletin, The, New York, 1923–

Ecclesiastical Review, The (originally *The American Ecclesiastical Review*), Philadelphia, 1889–

Ephemerides Liturgicae, Romae, 1887–

Gregorianum, Romae, 1920–

Homiletic and Pastoral Review, The, New York, 1900–

Irish Ecclesiastical Record, The, Dublin, 1864–

Jus Pontificium, Romae, 1921–

L'Ami du Clergé, Paris, 1878–

Monitore Ecclesiastico, Il, Romae, 1876–

Perfice Munus, Turin, 1926–

Periodica de Re Canonica et Morali, Brugis, 1905–; ab anno 1927: *Periodica de Re Canonica, Morali, Liturgica.*

Pastor, The, New York, 1882–1888.

Revue Ecclésiastique de Liége, Leodii, 1908–

Revue du Clergé Français, Paris, 1895–1920.

PRINCIPAL ARTICLES

Anonymous, "De L'Application De La Messe Pro Populo"—*Correspondance de Rome,* I (1848–1850), 107–125.

BRYS, J., "De Celebratione pro grege"—*Collationes Brugensis,* XXVIII (1928), 460–470.

CAPPELLO, F., "De Missa Pro Populo quando festum Annuntiationis B. M. V. incidat in feriam V, VI, vel Sabbatum hebdomadae maioris"—*Periodica,* XXI (1932), 146.

CLAEYS-BOUUAERT, F., "Quid statuatur per jus tum commune, tum particulare nostrum, circa obligationem parochorum missam celebrandi pro populo"—*Collationes Gandavenses,* XII (1925), 171–180.

KAISER, "Ecclesiastical Legislation on the Missa pro Populo"—*Ecclesiastical Review,* LXI (1919), 363-371.

LEROUX, E., "La Messe 'Pro Populo,'"—*Revue Ecclésiastique de Liége,* XIV (1922-1933), 148-157.

SLATER, T., "The Mass Pro Populo"—*Ecclesiastical Review,* LXII (1920), 634-640.

VERMEERSCH, A., "Applicatio Missae pro populo quando in die propria nequit applicari"—*Periodica,* XXI (1932) 162*-

————, "De Canoni 466 et de recta applicatione can. 6, 2°"—*Periodica,* XVII 1928), 136*-138*.

VILLIEN, A., "Les Curés Mobilisés et La Messe Pro Populo"—*Le Canoniste Contemporain,* XL (1917), 212-222.

ABBREVIATIONS

AAS—Acta Apostolicae Sedis.
ASS—Acta Sanctae Sedis.
CIC—Pontifical Commission for the Authentic Interpretation of the Code.
Coll. Lac.—Collectio Lacensis.
Coll. S.C.P.F.—Collectanea of the Sacred Congregation of the Propagation of the Faith.
CSEL—Corpus Scriptorum Ecclesiasticorum Latinorum.
ER—Ecclesiastical Review.
Fontes—Codicis Iuris Canonici Fontes cura . . . Gasparri editi.
Hardouin—*Acta Conciliorum,* etc.
HPR—Homiletic and Pastoral Review.
Mansi—*Sacrorum Conciliorum Nova et Amplissima Collectio.*
MPG—Migne, *Patrologia Graeca.*
MPL—Migne, *Patrologia Latina.*
Periodica—*Periodica de Re Canonica et Morali.*
S.C.C.—*Sacred Congregation of the Council.*
S.R.C.—*Sacred Congregation of Rites.*
Thesaurus—Sacrae Congregationis Concilii Resolutiones.

BIOGRAPHICAL NOTE

Thomas Andrew Donnellan was born January 24, 1914, in New York City, New York. His grammar school education was completed at Holy Family Parochial School, Bronx, New York. He was graduated from Regis High School and entered Cathedral College, the preparatory seminary of the Archdiocese of New York, receiving the degree of Bachelor of Arts from that institution. In the fall of 1933 he enrolled at St. Joseph's Seminary, Dunwoodie, New York, and was ordained to the Priesthood in New York City on June 3, 1939. In September of that year he entered the Catholic University of America to pursue a graduate course of studies. From this institution he received the degree of the Baccalaureate in Canon Law in June, 1940, and the degree of the Licentiate in Canon Law in June, 1941.

INDEX

CANON LAW STUDIES

1. Freriks, Rev. Celestine A., C.PP.S., J.C.D., Religious Congregations in Their External Relations, 121 pp., 1916.
2. Galliher, Rev. Daniel M., O.P., J.C.D., Canonical Elections, 117 pp., 1917.
3. Borowski, Rev. Aurelius L., O.F.M., J.C.D., De Confraternitatibus Ecclesiasticis, 136 pp., 1918.
4. Castillo, Rev. Cayo, J.C.D., Disertacion Historico-Canonica sobre la Potestad del Cabildo en Sede Vacante o Impedida del Vicario Capitular, 99 pp., 1919 (1918).
5. Kubelbeck, Rev. William J., S.T.B., J.C.D., The Sacred Penitentiaria and Its Relations to Faculties of Ordinaries and Priests, 129 pp., 1918.
6. Petrovits, Rev. Joseph J. C., S.T.D., J.C.D., The New Church Law on Matrimony, X-461 pp., 1919.
7. Hickey, Rev. John J., S.T.B., J.C.D., Irregularities and Simple Impediments in the New Code of Canon Law, 100 pp., 1920.
8. Klekotka, Rev. Peter J., S.T.B., J.C.D., Diocesan Consultors, 179 pp., 1920.
9. Wanenmacher, Rev. Francis, J.C.D., The Evidence in Ecclesiastical Procedure Affecting the Marriage Bond, 1920 (Printed 1935).
10. Golden, Rev. Henry Francis, J.C.D., Parochial Benefices in the New Code, IV-119 pp., 1921 (Printed 1925).
11. Koudelka, Rev. Charles J., J.C.D., Pastors, Their Rights and Duties According to the New Code of Canon Law, 211 pp., 1921.
12. Melo, Rev. Antonius, O.F.M., J.C.D., De Exemptione Regularium, X-188 pp., 1921.
13. Schaaf, Rev. Valentine Theodore, O.F.M., S.T.B., J.C.D., The Cloister, X-180 pp., 1921.
14. Burke, Rev. Thomas Joseph, S.T.D., J.C.D., Competence in Ecclesiastical Tribunals, IV-117 pp., 1922.
15. Leech, Rev. George Leo, J.C.D., A Comparative Study of the Constitution, "Apostolicae Sedis" and the "Codex Juris Canonici," 179 pp., 1922.
16. Motry, Rev. Hubert Louis, S.T.D., J.C.D., Diocesan Faculties According to the Code of Canon Law, II-167 pp., 1922.
17. Murphy, Rev. George Lawrence, J.C.D., Delinquencies and Penalties in the Administration and Reception of the Sacrament, IV-121 pp., 1923.
18. O'Reilly, Rev. John Anthony, S.T.B., J.C.D., Ecclesiastical Sepulture in the New Code of Canon Law, II-129 pp., 1923.

19. Michalicka, Rev. Wenceslas Cyrill, O.S.B., J.C.D., Judicial Procedure in Dismissal of Clerical Exempt Religious, 107 pp., 1923.
20. Dargin, Rev. Edward Vincent, S.T.B., J.C.D., Reserved Cases According to the Code of Canon Law, IV–103 pp., 124.
21. Godfrey, Rev. John A., S.T.B., J.C.D., The Right of Patronage According to the Code of Canon Law, 153 pp., 1924.
22. Hagedorn, Rev. Francis Edward, J.C.D., General Legislation on Indulgences, II–154 pp., 1924.
23. King, Rev. James Ignatius, J.C.D., The Administration of the Sacraments to Dying Non-Catholics, V–141 pp., 1924.
24. Winslow, Rev. Francis Joseph, A.F.M., J.C.D., Vicars and Prefects Apostolic, IV–149 pp., 1924.
25. Correa, Rev. Jose Servelion, S.T.D., J.C.D., La Potestad Legislativa de la Iglesia Catolica, IV–127 pp., 1925.
26. Dugan, Rev. Henry Francis, A.M., J.C.D., The Judiciary Department of the Diocesan Curia, 87 pp., 1925.
27. Keller, Rev. Charles Frederick, S.T.B., J.C.D., Mass Stipends, 167 pp., 1925.
28. Paschang, Rev. John Linus, J.C.D., The Sacramentals According to the Code of Canon Law, 129 pp., 1925.
29. Pointek, Rev. Cyrillus, O.F.M., S.T.B., J.C.D., De Indulto Exclaustrationis necnon Saecularizationis, XIII–289 pp., 1925.
30. Kearney, Rev. Richard Joseph, S.T.B., J.C.D., Sponsors at Baptism According to the Code of Canon Law, IV–127 pp., 1925.
31. Bartlett, Rev. Chester Joseph, A.M., LL.B., J.C.D., The Tenure of Parochial Property in the United States of America, V–108 pp., 1926.
32. Kilker, Rev. Adrian Jerome, J.C.D., Extreme Unction, V–425 pp., 1926.
33. McCormick, Rev. Robert Emmett, J.C.D., Confessors of Religious, VIII–266 pp., 1926.
34. Miller, Rev. Newton Thomas, J.C.D., Founded Masses According to the Code of Canon Law, VII–93 pp., 1926.
35. Roelker, Rev. Edward G., S.T.D., J.C.D., Principles of Privilege According to the Code of Canon Law, XI–166 pp., 1926.
36. Bakalarczyk, Rev. Richardus, M.I.C., J.U.D., De Novitiatu, VIII–208 pp., 1927.
37. Pizzuti, Rev. Lawrence, O.F.M., J.U.L., De Parochis Religiosis, 1927. (Not printed.)
38. Bliley, Rev. Nicholas Martin, O.S.B., J.C.D., Altars According to the Code of Canon Law, XIX–132 pp., 1927.
39. Brown, Mr. Brendan Francis, A.B., LL.M., J.U.D., The Canonical Juristic Personality with Special Reference to Its Status in the United States of America, V–212 pp., 1927.
40. Cavanaugh, Rev. William Thomas, C.P., J.U.D., The Reservation of the Blessed Sacrament, VIII–101 pp., 1927.

41. Doheny, Rev. William J., C.S.C., A.B., J.U.D., Church Property: Modes of Acquisition, X–118 pp., 1927.
42. Feldhaus, Rev. Aloysius H., C.PP.S., J.C.D., Oratories, IX–141 pp., 1927.
43. Kelly, Rev. James Patrick, A.B., J.C.D., The Jurisdiction of the Simple Confessor, X–208 pp., 1927.
44. Neuberger, Rev. Nicholas J., J.C.D., Canon 6 or the Relation of the Codex Juris Canonici to the Preceding Legislation, V–95 pp., 1927.
45. O'Keefe, Rev. Gerald Michael, J.C.D., Matrimonial Dispensations, Powers of Bishops, Priests and Confessors, VIII–232 pp., 1927.
46. Quigley, Rev. Joseph, A.M., A.B., J.C.B., Condemned Societies, 139 pp., 1927.
47. Zaplotnik, Rev. Johannes Leo, J.C.D., De Vicariis Foraneis, X–142 pp., 1927.
48. Duskie, Rev. John Aloysius, A.B., J.C.D., The Canonical Status of the Orientals in the United States, VIII–196 pp., 1928.
49. Hyland, Rev. Francis Edward, J.C.D., Excommunication, Its Nature, Historical Development and Effects, VIII–181 pp., 1928.
50. Reinmann, Rev. Gerald Joseph, O.M.C., J.C.D., The Third Order Secular of Saint Francis, 201 pp., 1928.
51. Schenk, Rev. Francis J., J.C.D., The Matrimonial Impediments of Mixed Religion and Disparity of Cult, XVI–318 pp., 1929.
52. Coady, Rev. John Joseph, S.T.D., J.U.D., A.M., The Appointment of Pastors, VII–150 pp., 1929.
53. Kay, Rev. Thomas Henry, J.C.D., Competence in Matrimonial Procedure, VIII–164 pp., 1929.
54. Turner, Rev. Sidney Joseph, C.P., J.U.D., The Vow of Poverty, XLIX–217 pp., 1929.
55. Kearney, Rev. Raymond A., A.B., S.T.D., J.C.D., The Principles of Delegation, VII–149 pp., 1929.
56. Conran, Rev. Edward James, A.B., J.C.D., The Interdict, V–163 pp., 1930.
57. O'Neil, Rev. William H., J.C.D., Papal Rescripts of Favor, VII–218 pp., 1930.
58. Bastnagel, Rev. Clement Vincent, J.U.D., The Appointment of Parochial Adjutants and Assistants, XV–257 pp., 1930.
59. Ferry, Rev. William A., A.B., J.C.D., Stole Fees, V–135 pp., 1930.
60. Costello, Rev. John Michael, A.B., J.C.D., Domicile and Quasi-domicile, VII–201 pp., 1930.
61. Kremer, Rev. Michael Nicholas, A.B., S.T.B., J.C.D., Church Support in the United States, VI–1930.
62. Angulo, Rev. Luis, C.M., J.C.D., Legislation de la Inglesia sobre la intencion en la application de la Santa Misa, VII–104 pp., 1931.
63. Frey, Rev. Wolfgang Norbert, O.S.B., A.B., J.C.D., The Act of Religious Profession, VIII–174 pp., 1931.
64. Roberts, Rev. James Brendan, A.B., J.C.D., The Banns of Marriage, XIV–140 pp., 1931.

65. Ryder, Rev. Raymond Aloysius, A.B., J.C.D., Simony, IX-151 pp., 1931.
66. Campagna, Rev. Angelo, Ph.D., J.U.D., Il Vicario Generale del Vescovo, VII-205 pp., 1931.
67. Cox, Rev. Joseph Godfrey, A.B., J.C.D., The Administration of Seminaries, VI-124 pp., 1931.
68. Gregory, Rev. Donald J., J.U.D., The Pauline Privilege, XV-165 pp., 1931.
69. Donohue, Rev. John F., J.C.D., The Impediment of Crime, VII-110 pp., 1931.
70. Dooley, Rev. Eugene A., O.M.I., J.C.D., Church Law on Sacred Relics, IX-143 pp., 1931.
71. Orth, Rev. Raymond Clement, O.M.C., J.C.D., The Approbation of Religious Institutes, 171 pp., 1931.
72. Pernicone, Rev. Joseph M., A.B., J.C.D., The Ecclesiastical Prohibition of Books, XII-267 pp., 1932.
73. Clinton, Rev. Connell, A.B., J.C.D., The Paschal Precept, IX-108 pp., 1932.
74. Donnelly, Rev. Francis B., A.M., S.T.L., J.C.D., The Diocesan Synod, VIII-125 pp., 1932.
75. Torrente, Rev. Camilo, C.M.F., J.C.D., Las Processiones Sagradas, V-145 pp., 1932.
76. Murphy, Rev. Edwin J., C.PP.S., J.C.D., Suspension Ex Informata Conscientia, XI-122 pp., 1932.
77. Mackenzie, Rev. Eric F., A.M., S.T.L., J.C.D., The Delict of Heresy in Its Commission, Penalization, Absolution, VII-124 pp., 1932.
78. Lyons, Rev. Avitus E., S.T.B., J.C.D., The Collegiate Tribunal of First Instance, XI-147 pp., 1932.
79. Connolly, Rev. Thomas A., J.C.D., Appeals, XI-195 pp., 1932.
80. Sangmeister, Rev. Joseph V., A.B., J.C.D., Force and Fear as Precluding Matrimonial Consent, V-211 pp., 1932.
81. Jaeger, Rev. Leo A., A.B., J.C.D., The Administration of Vacant and Quasi-vacant Episcopal Sees in the United States, IX-229 pp., 1932.
82. Rimlinger, Rev. Herbert T., J.C.D., Error Invalidating Matrimonial Consent, VII-79 pp., 1932.
83. Barrett, Rev. John, D.M., S.S., J.C.D., A Comparative Study of the Third Plenary Council of Baltimore and the Code, IX-221 pp., 1932.
84. Carberry, Rev. John J., Ph.D., S.T.D., J.C.D., The Juridical Form of Marriage, X-177 pp., 1934.
85. Dolan, Rev. John L., A.B., J.C.D., The Defensor Vinculi, XII-157 pp., 1934.
86. Hannan, Rev. Jerome D., A.M., S.T.D., LL.B., J.C.D., The Canon Law of Wills, IX-517 pp., 1934.
87. Lemieux, Rev. Delisle A., A.M., J.C.D., The Sentence in Ecclesiastical Procedure, IX-131 pp., 1934.
88. O'Rourke, Rev. James J., A.B., J.C.D., Parish Registers, VII-109 pp., 1934.

89. Timlin, Rev. Bartholomew, O.F.M., A.M., J.C.D., Conditional Matrimonial Consent, X–381 pp., 1934.
90. Wahl, Rev. Francis X., A.B., J.C.D., The Matrimonial Impediments of Consanguinity and Affinity, VI–125 pp., 1934.
91. White, Rev. Robert J., A.B., LL.B., S.T.B., J.C.D., Canonical Ante-Nuptial Promises and the Civil Law, VI–152 pp., 1934.
92. Herrera, Rev. Antonio Parra, O.C.D., J.C.D., Legislation Ecclesiastica sobra el Ayuno y la Abstinencia, XI–191 pp., 1935.
93. Kennedy, Rev. Edwin J., J.C.D., The Special Matrimonial Process in Cases of Evident Nullity, X–165 pp., 1935.
94. Manning, Rev. John J., A.B., J.C.D., Presumption of Law in Matrimonial Procedure, XI–111 pp., 1935.
95. Moeder, Rev. John M., J.C.D., The Proper Bishop for Ordination and Dismissorial Letters, VII–135 pp., 1935.
96. O'Mara, Rev. William A., A.B., J.C.D., Canonical Causes for Matrimonial Dispensations, IX–155 pp., 1935.
97. Reilly, Rev. Peter, J.C.D., Residence of Pastors, IX–81 pp., 1935.
98. Smith, Rev. Mariner T., O.P., S.T.L., J.C.D., The Penal Law for Religious, VII–169 pp., 1935.
99. Whalen, Rev. Donald W., A.M., J.C.D., The Value of Testimonial Evidence in Matrimonial Procedure, XII–297 pp., 1935.
100. Cleary, Rev. Joseph F., J.C.D., Canonical Limitations on the Alienation of Church Property, VIII–141 pp., 1936.
101. Glynn, Rev. John C., J.C.D., The Promoter of Justice, XX–337 pp., 1936.
102. Brennan, Rev. James H., S.S., A.M., S.T.B., J.C.D., The Simple Convalidation of Marriage, VI–135 pp., 1937.
103. Brunini, Rev. Joseph Bernard, J.C.D., The Clerical Obligations of Canons 139 and 142, X–121 pp., 1937.
104. Connor, Rev. Maurice, A.B., J.C.D., The Administrative Removal of Pastors, VIII–159 pp., 1937.
105. Guilfoyle, Rev. Merlin Joseph, J.C.D., Custom, XI–144 pp., 1937.
106. Hughes, Rev. James Austin, A.B., A.M., J.C.D., Witnesses in Criminal Trials of Clerics, IX–140 pp., 1937.
107. Jansen, Rev. Raymond J., A.B., S.T.L., J.C.D., Canonical Provisions for Catechetical Instruction, VII–153 pp., 1937.
108. Kealy, Rev. John James, A.B., J.C.D., The Introductory Libellus in Church Court Procedure, XI–121 pp., 1937.
109. McManus, Rev. James Edward, C.SS.R., J.C.D., The Administration of Temporal Goods in Religious Institutes, XVI–196 pp., 1937.
110. Moriarity, Rev. Eugene James, J.C.D., Oaths in Ecclesiastical Courts, X–115 pp., 1937.
111. Rainer, Rev. Eligius George, C.SS.R., J.C.D., Suspension of Clerics, XVII–249 pp., 1937.
112. Reilly, Rev. Thomas F., C.SS.R., J.C.D., Visitation of Religious, VI–195 pp., 1938.

113. Moriarty, Rev. Francis E., C.SS.R., J.C.D., The Extraordinary Absolution from Censures, XV–334 pp., 1938.
114. Connolly, Rev. Nicholas P., J.C.D., The Canonical Erection of Parishes, X–132 pp., 1938.
115. Donovan, Rev. James Joseph, J.C.D., The Pastor's Obligation in Prenuptial Investigation, XII–322 pp., 1938.
116. Harrigan, Rev. Robert J., M.A., S.T.B., J.C.D., The Radical Sanation of Invalid Marriages, VIII–208 pp., 1938.
117. Boffa, Rev. Conrad Humbert, J.C.D., Canonical Provisions for Catholic Schools, X–211 pp., 1939.
118. Parsons, Rev. Anscar John, O.M. Cap., J.C.D., Canonical Elections, XII–236 pp., 1939.
119. Reilly, Rev. Edward Michael, A.B., J.C.D., The General Norms of Dispensation, X–156 pp., 1939.
120. Ryan, Rev. Gerald Aloysius, A.B., J.C.D., Principles of Episcopal Jurisdiction, XII–172 pp., 1939.
121. Burton, Rev. Francis James, C.S.C., A.B., J.C.D., A Commentary on Canon 1125, X–222 pp., 1940.
122. Miaskiewicz, Rev. Francis Sigismund, J.C.D., Supplied Jurisdiction According to Canon 209, XII–340 pp., 1940.
123. Rice, Rev. Patrick William, A.B., J.C.D., Proof of Death in Prenuptial Investigation, VIII–156 pp., 1940.
124. Anglin, Rev. Thomas Francis, M.S., J.C.D., The Eucharistic Fast, VIII–183 pp., 1941.
125. Coleman, Rev. John Jerome, J.C.L., The Minister of Confirmation, VI–153 pp., 1941.
126. Downs, Rev. John Emmanuel, A.B., J.C.D., The Concept of Clerical Immunity, XI–163 pp., 1941.
127. Esswein, Rev. Anthony Albert, J.C.D., Extrajudicial Penal Powers of Ecclesiastical Superiors, X–144 pp., 1941.
128. Farrel, Rev. Benjamin Francis, M.A., S.T.L., J.C.D., The Rights and Duties of the Local Ordinary Regarding Congregations of Women Religious of Pontifical Approval, V–195 pp., 1941.
129. Feeney, Rev. Thomas John, A.B., S.T.L., J.C.D., Restitutio in Integrum, VI–169 pp., 1941.
130. Findlay, Rev. Stephen William, O.S.B., A.B., J.C.D., Canonical Norms Governing the Deposition and Degradation of Clerics, XVII–279 pp., 1941.
131. Goodwine, Rev. John, A.B., S.T.L., J.C.L., The Right of the Church to Acquire Property, VIII–119 pp., 1941.
132. Heston, Rev. Edward Louis, C.S.C., Ph.D., S.T.D., J.C.D., The Alienation of Church Property in the United States, XII–222 pp., 1941.
133. Hogan, Rev. James John, S.T.L., J.C.D., Judicial Advocates and Procurators, VIII–200 pp., 1941.
134. Kealy, Rev. Thomas M., A.B., Litt. B., J.C.D., Dowry of Women Religious, IX–152 pp., 1941.

135. Keene, Rev. Michael James, O.S.B., J.C.D., Religious Ordinaries and Canon 198, 1941.
136. Kerin, Rev. Charles A., S.S., M.A., S.T.B., J.C.D., The Privation of Christian Burial, XVI–279 pp., 1941.
137. Louis, Rev. William Francis, M.A., J.C.D., Diocesan Archives, X–109 pp., 1941.
138. McDevitt, Rev. Gilbert Joseph, A.B., J.C.D., Legitimacy and Legitimation, X–247 pp., 1941.
139. McDonough, Rev. Thomas Joseph, A.B., J.C.D., Apostolic Administrators, X–217 pp., 1941.
140. Meier, Rev. Carl Anthony, A.B., J.C.D., Penal Administrative Procedure Against Negligent Pastors, XI–240 pp., 1941.
141. Schmidt, Rev. John Rogg, A.B., J.C.D., The Principles of Authentic Interpretation in Canon 17 of the Code of Canon Law, XII–331 pp., 1941.
142. Slafkosky, Rev. Andrew Leonard, A.B., J.C.D., The Canonical Episcopal Visitation of the Diocese, X–197 pp., 1941.
143. Swoboda, Rev. Innocent Robert, O.F.M., J.C.D., Ignorance in Relation to the Imputability of Delicts, IX–271 pp., 1941.
144. Dubé, Rev. Arthur Joseph, A.B., J.C.D., The General Principles for the Reckoning of Time in Canon Law, VIII–299 pp., 1941.
145. McBride, Rev. James T., A.B., J.C.D., Incardination and Excardination of Seculars, XX–585 pp., 1941.
146. Król, Rev. John J., J.C.L., The Defendant in Contentious Trials.
147. Comyns, Rev. Joseph J., C.SS.R., J.C.L., The Papal and Episcopal Administration of Church Property.
148. Barry, Rev. Garrett Francis, O.M.I., J.C.L., Violation of the Cloister.
149. Bolduc, Rev. Gatien, C.S.V., A.B., S.T.L., J.C.L., Les études dans les religions cléricales.
150. Boyle, Rev. David John, M.A., J.C.L., The Juridic Effects of Moral Certitude on Pre-Nuptial Guarantees.
151. Canavan, Rev. Walter Joseph, M.A., Litt.D., J.C.L., Profession of Faith.
152. Desrochers, Rev. Bruno, A.B., Ph.L., S.T.B., J.C.L., Le Premier Concile Plénier de Québec et le Code de Droit Canonique.
153. Dillon, Rev. Robert Edward, A.B., J.C.L., Common Law Marriage.
154. Dodwell, Rev. Edward John, Ph.D., S.T.B., J.C.L., The Time and Place for the Celebration of Marriage.
155. Donnellan, Rev. Thomas Andrew, A.B., J.C.L., The Obligation of the Missa pro Populo.
156. Eltz, Rev. Louis Anthony, A.B., J.C.L., Co-operation in Crime.
157. Gass, Rev. Sylvester Francis, M.A., J.C.L., Ecclesiastical Pensions.
158. Guiniven, Rev. John Joseph, C.SS.R., J.C.L., The Precept of Hearing Mass on Sundays and Holy Days of Obligation.
159. Gulczynski, Rev. John Theophilus, J.C.L., The Desecration and Violation of Churches.

160. Hammill, Rev. John Leo, M.A., J.C.L., The Obligations of the Traveler According to Canon 14.
161. Haydt, Rev. John Joseph, A.B., J.C.L., Reserved Benefices.
162. Huser, Rev. Roger John, O.F.M., A.B., J.C.L., The Crime of Abortion in Canon Law.
163. Kearney, Rev. Francis Patrick, A.B., S.T.L., J.C.L., The Principles of Canon 1127.
164. Linahen, Rev. Leo James, S.T.L., J.C.L., De Absolutione Complicis in Peccato Turpi.
165. McCloskey, Rev. Joseph Aloysius, A.B., J.C.L., The Subject of Ecclesiastical Law according to Canon 12.
166. O'Neill, Rev. Francis Joseph, C.SS.R., J.C.L., The Dismissal of Religious in Temporary Vows.
167. Prince, Rev. John Edward, A.B., S.T.B., J.C.L., The Diocesan Chancellor.
168. Riesner, Rev. Albert Joseph, C.SS.R., J.C.L., Apostates and Fugitives from Religious Institutes.
169. Stenger, Rev. Joseph Bernard, J.C.L., The Mortgaging of Church Property.
170. Waldron, Rev. Joseph Francis, A.B., J.C.L., The Minister of Baptism.
171. Willett, Rev. Robert Albert, J.C.L., The Probative Value of Documents in Ecclesiastical Trials.
172. Woeber, Rev. Edward Martin, M.A., J.C.L., The Interpellations.

www.ingramcontent.com/pod-product-compliance
Lightning Source LLC
LaVergne TN
LVHW050210080826
844660LV00012B/388

* 9 7 8 0 8 1 3 2 2 3 4 4 5 *